UNLOCKING POWER IN THE DREAM DIMENSION:

THE PRINCIPLE OF FIRSTFRUIT

BY
CLARENCE E. MCCLENDON, PH.D.

UNLOCKING POWER IN THE DREAM DIMENSION:

THE PRINCIPLE OF FIRSTFRUIT

COPYRIGHT © 2003 BY CLARENCE E. MCCLENDON MINISTRIES

ISBN#: 1-59352-044-1

PUBLISHED BY:
CLARENCE E. MCCLENDON MINISTRIES
P.O. BOX 78398
LOS ANGELES, CA 90016

ALL RIGHTS RESERVED UNDER INTERNATIONAL COPYRIGHT LAW. CONTENTS AND/OR COVER MAY NOT BE REPRODUCED IN WHOLE OR IN PART IN ANY FOR WITHOUT WRITTEN CONSENT OF THE PUBLISHER.

UNLESS OTHERWISE INDICATED, ALL SCRIPTURE QUOTATIONS ARE FROM THE NEW KING JAMES VERSION, © 1979, 1980, 1982 BY THOMAS NELSON, INC.

SCRIPTURE QUOTATIONS MARKED (KJV) ARE FROM THE AUTHORIZED KING JAMES VERSION

PRINTED IN THE UNITED STATES OF AMERICA

COVER DESIGN BY:
LONNIE ROBINSON, QUICKSILVER
CREATIVE COMMUNICATIONS
5440 EXECUTIVE PL, SUITE F
JACKSON, MS 39206

Table of Contents

Acknowledgments v
Introduction vii

Chapter 1:

Giants in Dreamland 1
Ownership Precedes Occupancy
Occupancy Comes With Opposition
Giant Obstacles Signify Awesome Opportunities!

Chapter 2:

Breaking the Dream Barrier 7
It Is Not up to God, It Is up to You
Be Suspicious of Your Pain
Three Divine Principles

Chapter 3:

Downpayment in Dreamland 23
It Is Not Business As Usual
Know Your True Enemy

Chapter 4:

Financial Dominion in the dream Dimension 37
The Authority of Three
This Is a Covenant Matter
Invoke God's Power With the Tithe
Replenish and Exchange
How to Increase

CHAPTER 5:
CHRIST: THE FIRSTFRUIT 63

CHAPTER 6:
WHAT DOES LOVE HAVE TO DO WITH IT? 73
LOVE IS A KINGDOM PRINCIPLE
FORGIVENESS IS NOT AN ADMISSION OF WRONG
PEACE

CHAPTER 7:
MAKE YOUR DREAMS COME TRUE 87
EVIDENCE OF INCREASE
ANSWERS TO YOUR QUESTIONS

ABOUT THE AUTHOR... 97

**OTHER BOOKS
BY BISHOP CLARENCE E. MCCLENDON**...................... 99

Acknowledgments

- First, to my Lord and Savior, Jesus Christ, who anointed me to declare His truth. I am humbled to be charged with such a responsibility, and I thank Him for His continual grace upon my life so that I may make known the power of His gospel.

- To my wife, Priscilla, who continues to show me the joy of life. I thank you for sharing this work with me and encouraging me to do all that God has purposed.

- To my mother, Miriam, who helped raise me in the fear of the Lord. I am blessed by your strength and your example of humility.

- To the editing and research team at Siloam Bible College & Clarence E. McClendon Leadership Institute, thank you for your tireless effort to help produce the word of God. The Lord sees your heart and will reward your obedience.

- To the Clarence E. McClendon Ministries family, I thank God for your maturity in releasing me to fulfill the apostolic call of God on my life.

INTRODUCTION

At the end of the year 2001, I asked the Lord, "What shall I tell the people concerning the upcoming year? What do you want me to declare to Your people?" The Lord answered me and said, "Tell them that this is the year of the dream. I want My people to dare to dream in 2002." (And no matter what year it is when you read this book, this is God's word concerning you.) Now, lest you think your dream is too big, let me remind you that what you are carrying in your spirit is actually God's dream for you, for your family, for your business, for your life.

One thing you must come to understand about God is that He does not want you to merely exist in your dream. His desire is for you to have dominion in your dreamland. However, in order to do that you must know, understand and put into practice all He requires so your covenant with Him remains intact and His power is released to move you into your dream.

This is a matter of covenant. It is not a matter of ability or talent. It is not a matter of which church you attend or whose leadership you sit under. It is not a matter of your past. This is a matter of keeping covenant with God, who created you and chose you to bear fruit. Deuteronomy 8:18 declares, *"And you shall remember the Lord your God, for it is He who gives you power to get wealth, that He may* **establish His covenant** *which He swore to your fathers, as it is this day."*

The principle of firstfruits giving is something that the Spirit of the Lord placed in me some time ago, but He would not release me to declare it to the people until now. Dominion in your dream comes as a result of knowing your covenant with the Lord, and working it so that the fullness of His power is upon you. It is time for you to have dominion. God does not want you to move into your dreamland and be defeated for lack of knowledge.

One area of dominion in which Christians lack knowledge is their financial prosperity. There are three aspects of covenant given to the financial realm of the believer. They are the firstfruit, tithe and offering. I understand that we have only been taught two of the three, and as a result, our finances have experienced chaos and dysfunction. God established divine authority to fall in "threes." There are three lights ruling the skies: sun, moon and stars. Man is three parts: spirit, soul and body. The Godhead is three: Father, Son and Holy Spirit. There were three archangels in heaven: Gabriel, Michael and Lucifer. When one of them fell (Lucifer) chaos and disorder was the result.

By applying the principles outlined in this book, you will regain order in the financial area of your life so that God can bless you to the degree He desires. As the Lord begins to bless your obedience, I want you to write me and tell me all that God is doing in your life. I pray the Holy Spirit opens the eyes of your understanding and grants you revelation as you read. I pray you may know His power, and experience the tangible presence of God on your life and in your dream as you put this truth in its proper place.

CHAPTER I

GIANTS IN DREAMLAND

The Spirit of God spoke to me at the end of 2001 and said, "Tell the people that 2002 will be the 'Year of the Dream,'" and I began

> The **"Dream Dimension"** is God's dream for your life; it is God's promised place for you.

to preach about moving into the "dream dimension." The dream dimension is God's dream for your life, and if you are going to move into God's dream for your life you must understand that the dreams you have for the good things in your future are not yours. They are actually God's dreams for you. It is God who gives you dreams and visions of a better life, a better home, a better family, and a better business. God gives you those dreams because He wants you to live on a higher level. God wants you to prosper!

However, understanding that God gives you dreams and wants you to prosper is not enough. You also must understand there are three divine principles governing the dream dimension, God's

> **Divine Principles in the "Dream Dimension"**
> - Ownership precedes occupancy.
> - Occupancy comes with opposition.
> - Giant obstacles signify awesome opportunities!

promised place for you. The first principle is **ownership precedes occupancy**. The second is **occupancy comes with opposition**, and the third is **giant obstacles signify awesome opportunities**.

OWNERSHIP PRECEDES OCCUPANCY

Get accustomed to this because it is a divine principle. Ownership is spiritual authority. Occupancy is physical geography. Every time God moves you from this place to that dream place, every time He tells you to get up and move from your comfort zone to the promised zone, He is going to put you in a position where you are going to have to believe you own a thing before you occupy it. In other words, God transfers title in the spirit before He ever shows manifestation of occupancy in the natural.

In Numbers chapter 13, God tells Moses to *"send men to spy out the land of Canaan, which I am giving to the children of Israel."* When Moses sent the spies they saw giants and returned to Moses with a negative report. They did not understand that the giants **in** the land had nothing to do with who actually **owned** the land. God said, *"...the land of Canaan, which I am giving to the children of Israel..."* so it did not matter who was there or what they saw. The land was theirs because God said it was theirs. But remember, ownership always precedes occupancy and you must grow comfortable with that principle. You have to understand that there is a divine principle at work that says you own it before you live in it. God is in covenant with you, not your opposition. When He gives you something, you have to walk like it is yours and talk like it is yours. When you see the giants in your promised land you have to say to them, "God said this is mine, you just do not know it yet. Too bad, I am on my way in."

OCCUPANCY COMES WITH OPPOSITION

The second divine principle is that occupancy comes with opposition. I understand that facing an opposing force or obstacle affects us. Believe me, I know big problems can weigh on you—keep you up at night and cause you to pace the floor. They can make you cry sometimes when no one is around. They can cause you to complain, scratch your head, lock yourself alone in a room, and yell at the top of your lungs! There may even be times when you just have to get in the car and drive.

Understand, with opened doors there will be opposition, but here is the key. Just like giants in the land have nothing to do with who owns the land, the size of your obstacle has nothing to do with who has authority. There will always be giants in dreamland, but the size of your giants is irrelevant because size does not signify authority. The greatest authority in the earth is the living word of God Almighty. If you have God's word on the situation, there can be five Goliaths coming at you with swords and spears; but that uncircumcised Philistine has no chance against one who comes in the name of the Lord God of the armies of Israel. Your obstacle has no covenant with God. You are the one with the covenant, the promise, the blood of Jesus, the Word of God, and the Holy Ghost on your side.

GIANT OBSTACLES SIGNIFY AWESOME OPPORTUNITIES!

Understand that giant obstacles signify awesome opportunities. Your problems and your dreams will always be compatible in size. If you are wondering why obstacles are always hitting you, why hell is always breaking loose on you, it is because your dreams are so big. There are people who would love to have problems the size of yours because it is an indication of awesome dreams. Think about it. If you have a million-dollar need, you probably have a million-dollar dream!

The truth is the devil can do nothing to you if you start believing that greater is He who is in you than he that is in the world (1 John 4:4). Jesus did not die and shed His blood for a group of nobodies. If you are saved, you are somebody to God. If you are born again, you are somebody to God. If you are filled with the Holy Spirit, you are somebody to God. God would not waste His most precious gift, His Son. So, if you have the Holy Ghost, God sees something in your future and it is time to release the warrior inside you and go after it.

You may be wondering who this warrior is of whom I speak. He is the Lord, strong and mighty in battle. Some of you need to go into a phone booth like Clark Kent, take a dose of the Holy

Ghost and come out as Superman. You need to take off what you have on and put on your real clothes: the breastplate of righteousness and the helmet of salvation (Ephesians 6:14, 17). You need to put on your battle fatigues. It is time to go to war in the name of Jesus.

Remember, you are significant to God. You are important to God. When you come up against big problems, it is because you have big dreams. You have big obstacles because you have a big promise.

****

Now, Father, I plead the blood of Christ Jesus against the spirit of defeatism and the devil of deception. I command you, Satan, to loose my brother and let my sister go free. I command you in the name of Jesus! And I release that victory to you child of God, in the name of Jesus. I release grace by the power of the blood, and I declare that you are walking in it all day today, tomorrow, and every day, growing stronger and stronger as you meditate on God's Word.

Tell the enemy, "I am not an insect. You may look at me and think I am insignificant, but you have not seen anything yet. You do not know what is inside of me. I may appear nice, but you are going to see a side of me that will surprise us both. Behind this smiling face is a roaring lion, the lion of the tribe of Judah. Behind these eyes is a warrior. The real me is coming out. AMEN!"

CHAPTER II

BREAKING THE DREAM BARRIER

My assignment from God is that I give you the spiritual tools needed to move you in the direction of your dream. Before a year passes from the time you read this book you are to be moving in your dream, not simply talking about it. By the Spirit and the grace of God, you will be living in the manifestation of your dream. As mentioned in the first chapter, when God gives you big dreams you will experience equally big obstacles. To realize the full potential of God's dream for your life you must know how to overcome these obstacles. As I was meditating on this subject, the Spirit of God dealt with my heart and He told me, "Son, breaking the dream barrier is like breaking the sound barrier. You have to catch up to the speed of your dream. There will be some impediments, situations or circumstances that will hinder you from moving into that dimension."

In Joshua, chapter 3, the children of Israel cross over the Jordan. By chapter 5, they have already crossed over and we are given a post-facto account of their crossing. The Jordan was the barrier between the children of Israel and their dreamland. On one side of the Jordan lay their promised land. But they were living on the side in which they were free from bondage, but not possessing or living in their dream. Their situation is a type and shadow of the lives many of us are leading today. We are washed in the blood, forgiven of sin, saved, and on our way to Heaven; but we are not living in the fullness of the dream God gave us.

> *So it was, when all the kings of the Amorites who were on the west side of the Jordan, and all the kings of the Canaanites who were by the sea, heard that the Lord had dried up the waters of the Jordan from before the children of Israel until we had crossed over, that their*

> *heart melted; and there was no spirit in them any longer because of the children of Israel. At that time the Lord said to Joshua, "Make flint knives for yourself, and circumcise the sons of Israel again the second time." So Joshua made flint knives for himself, and circumcised the sons of Israel at the hill of the foreskins. And this is the reason why Joshua circumcised them: All the people who came out of Egypt who were males, all the men of war, had died in the wilderness on the way, after they had come out of Egypt. For all the people who came out had been circumcised, but all the people born in the wilderness, on the way as they came out of Egypt, had not been circumcised* (Joshua 5:1-5).

I thank God for my salvation, I am grateful that I am washed in the blood, and I rejoice that Jesus died for my sins, but I am not satisfied with just being saved. I want to be saved and live in the authority and the power of the dream God has for my life. The children of Israel were free and delivered, but they had not yet crossed over. They had not yet possessed the dream God gave to them.

IT IS NOT UP TO GOD, IT IS UP TO YOU

For 40 years before crossing over their barrier, the children of Israel lived by the Jordan but were unable to cross over it. In Numbers 13, God told the children of Israel to send spies out because He was giving them the land of Canaan.

> *And the Lord spoke to Moses, saying, "Send men to spy out the land of Canaan, which I am giving to the children of Israel; from each tribe of their fathers you shall send a man, every one a leader among them"* (Numbers 13:1-2).

Moses was obedient and sent 12 spies, one man from each tribe as God instructed. Immediately the spirits of defeatism and deception went to work and the spies returned with a negative report saying, *"We went to the land where you sent us. It truly flows with milk and honey, and this is its fruit. Nevertheless the people who dwell in the land are strong; the cities are fortified and very large; moreover we saw the descendants of Anak there"* (Numbers 13:27- 28). Because of the evil spirits of defeatism and deception, it took Israel 40 years to make what should have been an 11-day journey on foot.

What does this mean? It means crossing over your dream barrier is not up to God, it is up to you. God was ready to give Israel the land the moment He told them it was theirs, but they could not muster the strength or fortitude in the spirit to cross over and possess it. People are experiencing the same obstacles today. Someone reading this book is sick and tired of living next to a dream. Tired of being able to see it and taste it, but being unable to possess it. As God is my witness in Heaven above, someone reading this book is going to break through that barrier.

> **Divine Principles for Moving Into the "Dream Dimension"**
> - Consecrate yourself
> - Make a memorial
> - Renew your covenant responsibility

Continuing in the book of Joshua, God tells Joshua that he will take the children of Israel into their promised land. *"Moses my servant is dead. Now therefore, arise, go over this Jordan, you and all this people, to the land which I am giving to them – the children of Israel"* (Joshua 1:2). In chapter 2, Joshua also sends spies into the land of Canaan, but he only sent two. Remember, Moses sent 12. There is a revelation here. Joshua learned that sometimes you have to reduce your entourage in order to get your dream. Joshua only sent two spies into the land because he realized that too many cooks in the kitchen could spoil the dream.

As the story continues, we learn they scouted the land and stayed with Rahab, the harlot. In chapter 3, God begins to tell the children of Israel, "It is time;" time for them to stop living next to their dream and start living in it. It is time for you to stop living next to your dream and start living in it. It is time for you to stop talking about it and start moving in it. It is time for you to move all the excuses and kick all the devils out of the way and move into what God promised you.

God gave the children of Israel specific instructions. The Bible says that Joshua heard the word of God, and God told him, "It is time for you to cross over." God said He would send the Ark of the Covenant before them. The Ark of the Covenant represented God and the command was: *"When you see the ark of the Covenant of the Lord your God [crossing over the Jordan]...you shall set out from your place and go after it"* (Joshua 3:3).

BE SUSPICIOUS OF YOUR PAIN

When Paul says he is considering the suffering of this present time, as he examines his present circumstance, he recognizes something about the modality of God, the ways of God, the means by which God accomplishes things. The Bible says God *"made known His ways to Moses, His acts to the children of Israel"* (Psalm 103:7). The New Testament shows what God can do; the Old Testament tells you how He gets it done.

The book of Joshua says God commanded the children of Israel to leave a space between themselves and the Ark because they had not passed that way before. *"Yet there shall be a space between you and it, about two thousand cubits by measure. Do not come near it, that you may know the way by which you must go, for you have not passed this way before"* (Joshua 3:4). Now, that literally means when you are about to cross the dream barrier, you must give God some space to move the way He wants to move because He may not handle things in exactly the way in which you are accustomed. When you cross into a new dimension, you cannot *tell* God "I want a miracle just like this." You just tell Him, "God, do your thing and I will follow your Spirit anywhere you move." Therefore, Joshua teaches that when God moves, give Him some space.

As Paul contemplates his suffering, he recognizes a familiar pattern in how God works and when suffering comes, he lifts his hands to praise God. *"For I consider that the sufferings of this present time are not worthy to be compared with the glory which shall be revealed in us"* (Romans 8:18). Paul's suffering indicates to him that there is something behind the suffering more powerful than the suffering itself. *"For the **earnest expectation of the creation** eagerly waits for the revealing of the sons of God. For the creation was subjected to futility, not willingly, but because of Him who subjected it in hope"* (Romans 8:19-20).

"Earnest expectation" actually means down payment. For example, when you give someone **earnest** money, you are giving them evidence that you will be back to pay the rest and redeem your debt in full. Paul understands that God first makes a down payment, which is a promise. This down payment elevates your expectation to look for God to do something.

Someone reading this book is expecting something from God. God placed a dream in you and through His promise, His revelation and His word, your expectation came alive in your soul. Expectation is the breeding ground for miracles. When God gives you expectation, you begin to look different and walk different. It will cause you to go across town just because someone promised they were going to give you something. You have not seen it, you do not even know if they are sincere, but because they called you on the phone and told you they had something for you, you changed your whole attitude. Suddenly, you will do whatever you have to do to get what you have been expecting.

The problem is when God begins to agitate you with promise the enemy recognizes the expectation in you. You begin to shout a little louder, pray a little more earnestly, and shout the victory more frequently than usual. You come up on his radar because you have been impregnated with supernatural expectation. The enemy may not know exactly what God has for you, but he recognizes expectation rising in you. So, he sends a minion, an imp, or a little devil to agitate you and neutralize your expectation. He begins to agitate you so that your expectation begins to drop. He cannot stop the manifestation of God's promise in you, but if he can neutralize your expectation, then he can put off your manifestation even to another generation.

Understand that when God says something is going to happen, it is going to happen. The only question is, through whom. This is why Mordecai told Esther, deliverance is going to come from somewhere and if you get with the program God may use you. But, with or without you, deliverance will happen. You must make up your mind that you are not going to carry a baby for eight months and then let somebody else deliver it. You are the one who had the morning sickness, you are the one who had strange cravings. Do not allow the enemy to neutralize your expectation.

When you understand the ways of God you become suspicious of the pain caused by your circumstances. You realize that you would not experience this kind of pain unless there was something on the other side greater than your suffering. If God's promise was small, the enemy would not be fighting against you so hard. Because your promise from God is glorious, powerful and mighty, the suffering seems heavy. Understand how God does things. The Bible says the creation was subjected to futility, not because God wanted it to be but because He understood that futility produces hope. It is like submerging a ball filled with air under water. The more you sink it down, the harder it springs back up. You have a right to expect resurrection in your situation. It does not come by might or by power, but by My Spirit says the Lord of Hosts. God will raise you up. The lower you are knocked down, the higher you will rise. God wants you to know there is glory on the other side, not just spiritual glory, but wealth and money.

Someone reading this book is suspicious. You have considered your suffering, and it has educated you. You have seen the same thing happen before and the last time you almost let the devil convince you that you could not do something you were already doing. It is amazing how the enemy tries to convince you that you cannot do something you are already doing. You have been praising God without money for weeks, believing He would bless you. You have been rejoicing riding the bus for months, declaring God's promises. You have been carrying a heavy burden, still coming to church and shouting hallelujah every chance you get! You have been hit so many times, there is nowhere left to hit you. Then the enemy tries to convince you that you are not going to make it. The fact is, you have been making it all along. Do not allow the devil to convince you that you cannot do what you are already doing.

I encourage you to read the Old Testament to learn the ways of God. The Old Covenant contains types and shadows written for our example to show us how God manipulates situations, orchestrates enemies, lifts one up and takes another down, and moves obstacles opposing His purpose out of the way to get a job done. My God has the ability to turn a situation around in the nick of time. He can make what looks like a mess up turn into a bless up.

THREE DIVINE PRINCIPLES:
1. CONSECRATE YOURSELF

God began to deal with my heart about His instructions to Israel, which enabled them to cross the barrier into their dream dimension and their land. Notice the first thing God says to Israel in Joshua 3:5, "And Joshua said to the people, *"Sanctify yourselves, for tomorrow the Lord will do wonders among you."* The Spirit of God impressed upon me that there is a miracle in our immediate

> **"Sanctify"** literally means to consecrate yourself; separate yourself from the usual and the regular; to distinguish yourself from what you usually do.

futures—yours and mine. It is already set up. It is already prepared. Joshua says to *"sanctify yourselves, for tomorrow..."* implying it was already done. In other words, God was always prepared to do it. Sanctify literally means to consecrate. God is saying that consecration is necessary if you are going to break the dream barrier. This is an important concept that you must understand. But more than that, I want you to expand your definition of consecration. When we hear sanctify or consecrate yourself, we immediately think: "Well I just have to be holy. I cannot make a mistake. If I do anything wrong then it is all over."

Understand this definition is not exclusively what God means when He says consecrate. You are never going to be so flawless that you merit the goodness of God. You are never going to live without doing something for which you need to repent. You are not flawless. When God says consecrate yourselves, He does not call you to unblemished perfection. Consecrate means to distinguish yourself from what you usually do. God wants you to adopt a mindset in which you separate yourself from the usual, regular, ordinary, and mundane. It is this mindset in which Paul wrote to Timothy saying: *"No one engaged in warfare entangles himself with the affairs of this life, that he may please him who enlisted him as a soldier"* (2 Timothy 2:4).

> **Divine Principle**
>
> To see something different in your future, you must do something different in your present.

This is the principle: if you want to see something different in your future, you must do something different in your present. You cannot keep acting the sameway and expect to break through a barrier. So, however this applies to your life, you must separate from the ordinary, the regular. You must do whatever it takes to focus on achieving your dream. Remember, as we discussed in chapter 1, the dream I am referring to is really God's dream for your future, your life, His promised place for you. In other words, you must eliminate anything that keeps you from pursuing God's dream for your life.

Change your daily activity and modality. Divorce yourself from the unclean and the usual. Unexpected power is released when you consecrate yourself. The act of consecration will release in your situation power that is necessary, but unanticipated by you. Joshua chapter 5 says that the kings of the Amorites and the Canaanites were afraid of the children of Israel when they heard what God had done for them in drying up the Jordan.

> *So it was, when all the kings of the Amorites who were on the west side of the Jordan, and all the kings of the Canaanites who were by the sea, heard that the Lord had dried up the waters of the Jordan from before the children of Israel until we had crossed over, that their heart melted; and there was no spirit in them any longer* (Joshua 5:1).

Those were the same kings that were there for 40 years. The same giants that were in the land had been there for 40 years. So what was different now? God took the people's eyes off the giants and put them on the Ark of the Covenant. Their eyes were now off the impediment and on the Spirit of God. When they consecrated themselves, God released the power they needed but were not anticipating. While you are worried about your enemies, there is unexpected power that God is releasing. Once God releases His power, your enemies are going to be worried about you. When you consecrate yourself, God releases power you did not even realize you needed. I dare you to step toward God and watch what He will do on your behalf.

God tells you to consecrate yourself because He already has the devil's knees knocking. God tells you to shut down, fast, pray another hour, or turn the TV off because He has already gone into the devil's camp and blown them out of the water. He just needs someone in the natural realm to believe and take action. *"It is not by might nor by power, but by my Spirit says the Lord of Hosts"* (Zechariah 4:6).

2. Make A Memorial

By Joshua chapter 4, the children of Israel cross over and receive their second instruction from God. The second thing He calls Israel to do is to make a memorial for future generations.

And it came to pass, when all the people had completely crossed over the Jordan, that the Lord spoke to Joshua, saying: "Take for yourselves twelve men from the people, one man from every tribe, and command them, saying, 'Take for yourselves twelve stones from here, out of the midst of the Jordan, from the place where the priests' feet stood firm. You shall carry them over with you and leave them in the lodging place where you lodge tonight'...that this may be a sign among you when your children ask in time to come, saying, 'What do these stones mean to you? 'Then you shall answer them that the waters of the Jordan were cut off before the ark of the covenant of the Lord; when it crossed over the Jordan the waters of the Jordan were cut off. And these stones shall be for a memorial to the children of Israel forever."...Then he spoke to the children of Israel, saying: "When your children ask their fathers in time to come, saying: 'What are these stones?' Then you shall let your children know, saying 'Israel crossed over this Jordan on dry land': for the Lord your God dried up the waters of the Jordan before you until you had crossed over, as the Lord your God did to the Red Sea, which He dried up before us until we had crossed over, that all the peoples of the earth may know the hand of the Lord, that it is mighty, that you may fear the Lord your God forever" (Joshua 4:1-3, 6-7, 21-24).

God says that in order to cross over – to break the dream barrier – you must consecrate yourself and memorialize the event. First, God caused the children of Israel to cross over the Jordan, telling Joshua that when the priests carrying the Ark put their feet in the waters of the Jordan, the Jordan would dry up. Then, when it came to pass just as God said, He told them not to forget what happened. He told them to make a memorial of the event for future generations.

In the last 12 months, I am sure God has done something for you. You need to take 20 or 30 minutes and write down what He has taught you in the wilderness, because you are going to need it in a few days. This is evidence that the God you serve is **able**. God has done something for you that you must make the devil remember. He is doing something for you today that you will need to remember in the future. Memorialize it.

When the enemy said you would never make it, God broke through at the last minute. There is someone reading this book that a doctor told would never get well and God healed you. There is someone reading this book that was going to be evicted, and just in the nick of time, God provided. Write it down. When the enemy tells you "you are not going to make it," you say, "Devil, check this out, do you remember this?"

Put it in your Bible. Put it on your refrigerator. Put it on your mirror. Every once in a while, you need to remind the devil that when he thought he had you locked down, beat down, thrown down, and put out, you praised God. The more the enemy attacked, the more you praised God. Remember it and remind the enemy. Remember those nights you prayed all night long because you needed an answer by early morning and suddenly you got an unexpected phone call from somebody – unexpected, but right on time.

Someone reading this book needs to go back into the history of God's dealings in their life. There is someone who should have been dead and in their grave. There are friends of yours who did not make it out of what you survived. Write it down and remind the devil that your God has a reputation for pulling things out just in time. He is the God who did it once and will do it again. It does not matter if the situation is different; God is the same. It does not matter if the devil is bigger; God is the same. It does not matter if you need more money today than you did last year; God is the same. The Bible says, *"He knows how to deliver the Godly out of temptation"* (2 Peter 2:9). So, whatever you do, stay Godly.

3. RENEW YOUR COVENANT RESPONSIBILITY

The last instruction God gave to Joshua before the children of Israel crossed over was to circumcise all the male children of Israel who had not been circumcised in the wilderness (Joshua 5:2). The children of Israel had been in the wilderness for 40 years and they had not circumcised any of the male children. Circumcision was part of their covenant responsibility with God and they grew complacent in keeping their covenant. There was a whole generation born in the wilderness who had not been circumcised. God said they must renew their covenant before they could move completely into their dreamland.

Now this does not mean that you must go through a painful situation in order to break the dream barrier. What it does mean is that you must renew your covenant responsibility. I know you have been under attack. I know you have been hit where it hurts, but you must pull it together and get back to carrying out your covenant responsibilities. Get up, wash your face, tie your shoes, put on your coat, stop walking around on your lips, and start lifting up your voice like a child of God. Look in the mirror and tell yourself to get it together. *"Weeping may endure for a night, but joy comes in the morning,"* (Psalms 30:5b). Your morning is here.

Lift up your voice and bless the name of the Lord. God says that He wants us to get back to our covenant responsibility. It is not your intellect that will win the battle. It is keeping your covenant. So, if you have stopped tithing, start tithing again. If you have stopped praying, start praying again. If you have lost your praise in the wilderness, find it again and say, *"I will bless the Lord at all times. His praise shall continually be in my mouth"* (Psalms 34:1).

Lift up holy hands, fast, praise, and believe God. Get your consecration back. Tell God you know you slipped a little but you want your anointing back. Do like Peter did when he was in the dungeon. In Acts 12 the Bible says that he was asleep and the angel woke him up and said listen, before you get out of here, put on your sandals and gird yourself. In other words, if you really mean it this time, show God you are ready to move out of where you are and into your dream.

You may wonder how God knows when you are ready to move into your dream. He knows when you praise Him even though you do not feel like it; when you tithe even though you are almost broke; when you dance even though everyone tells you not to. The Bible says that Miriam danced with a tambourine, and David danced with all his might when the Ark of the Covenant came back to Israel. You need to know that an outward expression of praise is universal. It is a Holy Ghost inspired redemption thing. Others may look at you and wonder what is wrong with you. Just tell them you are giving God evidence that you are ready to leave where you are and move into your dream. Child of God, there is something that you need but have not quite anticipated. God is prepared to bring you through. You have been next to a barrier that you have been unable to cross. God is giving you the power today to cross that barrier. That addiction is turning you loose today. That torment is leaving you today. It is the power of God that is accomplishing it, and all He needs is your obedience.

****

Father, in the name of Jesus, I pray for my brother and my sister. I thank You, Lord, for the courage and confidence of the Holy Spirit. I decree, by reason of the anointing, a barrier-breaking move of the Holy Ghost concerning my brother's dream and my sister's dream, in the name of Jesus.

Satan, get out of their way! Your time is up. You know it, now they know it. I release a miracle, a physical manifestation of God on their behalf. I declare in the name of Jesus, there is a miracle in their immediate future. Amen!

CHAPTER III

DOWNPAYMENT IN DREAMLAND

About two and a half years ago the Lord spoke to my heart about something that I was doing out of obedience to Him but did not realize was an ordinance of His. I walked in it only as an aspect of revelation. In other words, God told me to do a particular thing at various times, and I obeyed Him because I obey His voice. But, I did not realize I was obeying something that was a decree of God. When I found out it was an ordinance, the Lord told me that if I would put this action in place with the rest of what He had already given me, I would experience another dimension of personal release, dominion and prosperity. It has happened. As the economy has gone down and my church's economy went through a serious period, I continued to prosper. It was not because I was stealing. It was because I obeyed God.

As I walked in this revelation, I asked God to please let me tell someone and He released me to tell two people in my church. They began to prosper to such a degree and God revealed to me that one of them would become a millionaire within 12 months! This is so significant that once it is put in place in your life, you will break through into a new dimension of relationship and blessing in God.

After walking in this for almost two and a half years, I was scheduled to preach at a conference and the Lord instructed me to arrive a day early. This is unusual for me because I have a busy schedule and when I travel to preach, I generally arrive in time to minister, get in and get right back out again. But this time, God told me to arrive a day early. I did not know why God wanted me there early until I heard the man of God ministering about the very thing God put in my spirit almost a year prior but would not allow me to teach. Those of you who are really serious about moving into your dream are going to take this information, put it in its proper place and watch God break through barriers and establish dominion in your life. Because God released me to share this revelation with you, I am responsible for giving you everything you need to have dominion over the enemy. God holds me responsible for your lack. That is how serious the call of God is.

IT IS NOT BUSINESS AS USUAL

Now Jericho was securely shut up because of the children of Israel; None went out and none came in. And the Lord said to Joshua: "See! I have given Jericho into your hand, with its king and the mighty men of valor. You shall march around the city, all you men of war you shall go all around the city once. This you shall do six days.... But it came to pass on the seventh day that they rose early, about the dawning of the day, and marched around the city seven times in the same manner. On that day only they marched around the city seven times. And the seventh time it happened, when the priests blew the trumpets, that Joshua said to the people: "Shout, for the Lord has given you the city! Now the city shall be doomed by the Lord to destruction, it and all who are in it. Only Rahab the harlot shall live, she and all who are with her in the house, because she hid the messengers that we sent. And you, by all means abstain from the accursed things [the things that are doomed to destruction] lest you become accursed when you take of the accursed things, and make the camp of Israel a curse and trouble it. But all the silver and gold, and vessels of bronze and iron, are consecrated to the Lord; they shall come into the treasury of the Lord" (Joshua 6:1-3, 15-19).

Joshua declares to the children of Israel the manner in which God tells them to claim the city of Jericho. He begins by saying, "Shout, for the Lord has given you the city!" It is imperative to note that the people did not shout immediately. They waited for the rest of their instruction because those ordinances were going to take them into their dreamland.

The children of Israel crossed the Jordan and were about to fight their first battle, having crossed into the land of their dreams. This is their "down payment in dreamland." Back in Joshua 5, when Israel crossed over the Jordan, God sends them specific signals to signify things had changed.

As I mentioned in the last chapter, God instructed the children of Israel to renew their covenant before crossing into their dreamland by circumcising all those who had been born in the wilderness. After crossing over, they stayed in Gilgal until they were healed. They kept the Passover covenant and the Bible says they ate the fruit of the land. They had been in the wilderness, but now they were in the dream dimension—the land God promised them. They were living in the wilderness with no fruit, no bread, nothing green, just dry wilderness. They crossed over into dreamland and the first thing they saw was a land abundant with fruit—pomegranates, apples and grapes. So they went and ate the fruit of the land. The next day the manna ceased!

For 40 years the children of Israel were used to eating without knowing from where their sustenance came. They did not have to work for it. They did not have to know anything to get it. It was just there, every single day. Basically, it was divine, supernatural welfare. The term "manna" literally means, "what is it?" The children of Israel did not know where it came from or what caused it to come, so they named it "what is it?"

God is signaling to you that things have changed; things are different for you right now. You are no longer able to count on things you counted on in the past. God is not angry with you, but you are about to move into a dimension of dominion in the things

He put in your life, in your heart and in your spirit. You will not only live in your dream, you will dominate your dream dimension. You will not be just another businessman. You will be one of the most successful businessmen in your community. You will not have just any house. You will have your dream house. Your family is not going to be just another family. It is going to be a unique family that will be remembered. You are about to have dominion in your dream.

Once you move into your dream dimension, God will no longer sustain you in ignorance. God told me to tell you your manna is done! That is why some of you have seen your provisions shut down in the last few weeks and months. Some of you are experiencing shortages right now. It is not because you are out of God's will, it is because you have stepped over into the dream dimension and now God is moving you from welfare to work! Understand it is a great promise, but it is also a great responsibility.

It is not a bad thing. It is a signal that you have crossed over. Your lack today is not a signal that you are outside of the will of God, it is a signal that you are in His will and you are about to break through. In Joshua 6:1 the Bible says that Jericho was securely shut up because of the children of Israel. In other words the city was shut down because they heard the children of Israel coming, and your enemies—spirits of lack, poverty and depression—have shut down your provision because they heard you were coming. They shut down because they heard about what God did for you in parting the Red Sea to get you here. There has been communication in the demonic realm regarding people who are crossing over and taking dominion of their dreams. The enemy determines that the only way to stop them is to shut down their provisions in order to convince them they are out of the will of God.

And it came pass, when Joshua was by Jericho, that he lifted his eyes; and looked, and behold, a Man stood opposite him with His sword drawn in his hand. And Joshua went to Him and said to Him, "Are you for us or for our adversaries?" (Joshua 5:13).

If you have ever heard me preach or teach on this, you know this is one of my favorite verses. Joshua asks a man (who is actually an angel of the Lord) if he is for them or for their adversaries, and the man says "No." I want you to get this. He asks the man if he is for them or against them and the man says "No," he is neither for them nor against them. In other words, it is not a personal thing. God is not for you or your adversaries. He is for His purpose. If you cooperate with His purpose, He will fight for you. If you reject His purpose, he will oppose you. It is not personal. It does not matter what family you belong to, which church you attend, which Bishop you sit under, or whose television program you watch. It is not about that. It is about whether or not you are for God's purpose. Do you just want to get rich or do you want to establish His Kingdom? Do you just want to be seen or do you want to give glory to God? Do you just want a new house or do you want to be a witness that the God of the armies of Israel fought for you? It is not a personal thing. It is a Kingdom thing – Kingdom business!

Israel never fought any battles. They were not an army. They were a rag-tag bunch of slaves that did not know anything about warfare. They were carpenters, farmers, pyramid builders, and construction workers. They were freshly delivered slaves. The fact that they were not warriors was a prophetic statement. God was changing them from wanderers to warriors. Just like the children of Israel, you will have to become a warrior and you do not have a choice. If you want to walk in your dream, you have to become a part of the army! Put away your map and put on your fatigues!

God is signaling something to you and your adversaries. Things have shut down because of you. Your enemies have heard what God has done for you and they know you are coming.

Joshua 5, 9, 10, and 11 all begin with passages about the kings of the land having heard about what God did for Israel. Understand that every time you win there is a bulletin in hell communicating your victory and your adversaries know you are coming. So, once you defeat Sickness, Sickness calls Lack and says, "They beat me, but if you hit them in the next three or four weeks I think we can still keep them out of their dream." Once you defeat Lack, Lack calls Depression and says, "They got past me, but if you and Greed hit them we can keep them out." Your enemies have bound themselves together to defeat you and now you will win by warfare, not by manna. You are in the army now. You will not be ignorant anymore.

Know Your True Enemy

Though your dream may seem to have huge obstacles and huge giants against it, you must learn to keep your focus on the true enemy. The giants did not keep Israel out of Canaan. There was never a spear thrown or a sword lifted. There was never a gathering of armies. So it was not the giants who kept the children of Israel out of their dream, it was the attack of two evil spirits: Defeatism and Deception. Those same two spirits are at work today battling to keep you and me out of our dream dimensions.

> The giants did not keep the children of Israel out of their dreamland. It was the spirits of **defeatism** and **deception**.

In Numbers 13:31 the Bible says that when they saw giants in their promised land the spies reported, "We are not able to go up against the people." Notice the terminology. They did not say they were not able to fight the giants or that they did not have a chance to win. They were not even thinking about fighting. They said they were not able to go up against the giants. In other words, they were so defeated in their minds that they would not even lift up their swords to fight. This is a defeatist devil that concedes a battle even before there is any confrontation. The spirit of defeatism convinces you that it is too hopeless to even try. It has no place on a child in the Kingdom of God!

If God said it (in this case that the children of Israel would occupy the land of Canaan), then all He is looking for is someone who will stand in the face of Goliath and say, "Hit me with your best shot." While everyone else is saying, "He is too big to hit," you are saying "He is too big to miss." Regardless of the circumstances, you must remember that you are a child of the Most High God and there are no giants too big for God to handle. You may only have a slingshot, but it is loaded with a Holy Spirit guided missile. You do not even have to aim very well, just turn it loose. You do not even have to know which devil it is, just speak the Word of God and whichever devil it is, it is defeated.

The second spirit that kept Israel out of their promised land was the spirit of deception. *"There we saw the giants (the descendants of Anak came from the giants); and we were like grasshoppers in our own sight, and so we were in their sight"* (Numbers 13:33). The spirit of deception is a big, bold devil—a lie from the pit of hell that needs to be exposed. The spirit of deception tries to make you think of yourself as small and insignificant, nothing to be reckoned with. Think about it. These men went in as spies. If you are a spy, it means you are going undercover, not to be seen, camouflaged to hide. The lie of deception the devil told the children of Israel was two-fold. First, he convinced them that the enemy saw them and second, he made them believe they were seen as grasshoppers. The fact was, the enemy did not see them at all.

Likewise, your enemies will try to convince you that they see you as nothing. I assure you, if you could enter into demonic discussion and go behind the veil into Satan's war room to hear him giving his troops a pep talk, you would hear him say something like, "Whatever you do, do not let them believe that they are actually children of God. Whatever you do, do not let them believe that the blood of Jesus really has power. Do not let them believe that if they pray, God will answer. Do not let them lift up their hands and say 'Hallelujah.' Whatever you do, do not let them speak the name of Jesus. Do whatever you can to stop them, because if they ever pray, if they ever praise, if they ever start calling the name of Jesus, there is nothing we can do to stop them."

The fact is, the devil is afraid of your weapons. That is why he tries to keep you out of the fight. He knows if you ever suit up, he is going down. This deception is a lie. While you are staying up nights thinking your enemy can do this or that, the fact is your enemies probably have not thought of you at all. But they are about to have a few good thoughts because while you think God is dormant, things are going wrong in your enemy's world. Your enemies do not realize it yet, but God is moving on your behalf. God blesses those who bless you and curses those who curse you. That is how significant you are. That is how important you are to God. Your enemies are about to see the real you. Man! I prophesy that what is going to come out of you in the next few days is going to surprise even you. One of the things I love about God is that if you stay hooked up—intimately connected to Him—He will let it look to others like you did what it took to handle your situation. That is the kind of thing God does. As long as you acknowledge Him and give Him thanks, God makes you look good!

First, this warfare is not with your adversary. It is not with your enemy. God will take care of your enemy. Your battle is with your opinions, your actions and your emotions. That is the lesson God will teach you in a very significant way. When God tells you what to do and it does not make sense, you are going to have to decide whether you are going to obey your opinion or God's Word. In this dream dimension, Israel was about to fight, but their battle was not with Jericho! Remember, God told them to march around the city and they knew that marching around the city was not the way to defeat an army!

> **Divine Principal of Warfare in the "Dream Dimension"**
> Your battle is not with your adversary; it is with your emotions, opinions and actions.

For we do not wrestle against flesh and blood, but against principalities, against powers, against the rulers of the darkness of this age, against spiritual hosts of wickedness in the heavenly places. Therefore take up the whole armor of God, that you may be able to withstand in the evil day, and having done all, to stand (Ephesians 6:12-13).

Imagine the conversation. They probably thought; "We should put a spear in the hands of every man, woman, baby, dog, and parakeet. We can storm these folks at night when they are not looking. We need everybody to take up arms and just storm them." But Joshua tells them, "I understand that, but the Commander met with me last night and He gave me instructions. I know this is not how you take a city but the Commander instructed us to quietly march around the city for six days. You are going to have to battle with your emotions—be quiet when I tell you to be quiet, speak when I tell you to speak—and on the seventh day I want you to shout, but not until I tell you to shout. You are going to want to say something. You will want to retaliate when someone hits you. You will want to break ranks when someone offends you. You may get depressed and want to give up. The question is, are you going to follow your opinion on warfare or do what the Commander says?"

Remember, Joshua did not know anything about warfare. All he ever did was serve Moses, and write down what Moses said. If Moses needed his chariot washed, Joshua went and did that. He picked up Moses' dry cleaning and anytime Moses had anything to say Joshua just came and said it. What does he know about warfare? But God tells Joshua to tell the children of Israel that the Commander instructed them to march around for six days and be quiet. God wanted to teach them that it is not their might that wins battles in the dream dimension, it is **obeying His word**. Basically, God was saying that it did not matter whether or not their opinion contradicted His Word. Their battle was not with the obstacle in front of them, it was with their opinion.

Second, Joshua told the children of Israel to be quiet and keep their emotions in check. Can you be quiet when you are supposed to be quiet? Can you talk when somebody tells you to talk? If God tells you to praise in the midst of a depressed situation, can you do that? If God sends His word to you and tells you to give everything you have when all you have is $10, can you do that? God gives Joshua the instruction, and in turn, Joshua gives the instruction to the people of God.

> *And on the seventh day it happened, when the priest blew the trumpets, that Joshua said to the people "Shout, for the Lord has given you the city. Now the city shall be doomed by the Lord to destruction"* (Joshua 6:16-17).

****

Father, in the name of Jesus, help your people to put this truth into effect in their lives, not just today, but every day.

Father, in the name of Jesus, let the blessing of the firstfruit offering, the revelation of the spirit of truth and the breakthrough of the firstfruit, let it now come on my brother, my sister, on his house, on her house, on his business, on her business, on his family, on her family. I decree in Jesus' name that because of your obedience, you shall increase on the right hand and on your left hand. And you shall no more be defeated in your dreams. But the Lord will fight for you.

Now, in the name of Jesus, I declare that the enemies that have defeated you are now subject to you through the authority of the name of Jesus and your obedience to the covenant that He has given you for dominion in this area. Lack, you will no longer rule this man. Poverty, you will no longer prevail over that woman or her house. In the name of Jesus, as you put the word of God into effect, I bless you with the blessing of increase and I decree this blessing rests on your house as you obey Him.

Chapter IV

Financial Dominion in the Dream Dimension

In the previous chapters we looked at the divine principles you need to know in order to take ownership of your dream. In this chapter, we will unlock the principles essential to increasing in dominion and power in the dream dimension.

The principle of the Firstfruit offering is a truth that God is restoring to the body of Christ. Although it is not new from God's standpoint, it is a new principle for the people of God. We are to be personal witnesses to the fact that our God is a prospering God, one who blesses His people. The Lord chose to restore this truth to the church in the last days because there is no way the church will advance into the dimension of increase, prosperity and wealth required to finance the end-time harvest without it. The church will not reach that level of prosperity unless she puts into place all of the things God gives for her well being.

God began to reveal this revelation to me as I studied this part of our covenant with Him. He said, "Son, this is something I am restoring to the household of faith so that My people who are believing Me can reap the end-time harvest – increasing day by day, not just barely breaking even." Child of God, I want you to understand that this is not just about financial prosperity. This has to do with the end-time harvest. It is important for you to understand that.

Further, it has to do with you, as a child of God, coming into the dimension of your dream. This has to do with the area He has shown you that you are supposed to live in, possess, have, or be. It is whatever God told you concerning your dream. He is giving this truth so that we can establish dominion in the dream dimension and so that, as we come into His promises, we are not defeated for lack of knowledge.

Our foundational text for this chapter is Leviticus 23:9-12. It reads:

> *And the Lord spoke to Moses, saying, "Speak to the children of Israel, and say to them: 'When you come into the land which I give to you, and reap its harvest, then you shall bring a sheaf of the firstfruits of your harvest to the priest. He shall wave the sheaf before the Lord, to be accepted on your behalf; on the day after the Sabbath the priest shall wave it. And you shall offer on that day, when you wave the sheaf, a male lamb of the first year, without blemish, as a burnt offering to the Lord.'"*

There are several different levels on which we will dissect this passage of scripture. In verse 10, the Lord instructs Moses to declare to the children of Israel, "When you come into the land..." In other words, this is as important when you actually come into your dreamland as it is before you enter your dreamland. It is a principle that is eternal and necessary all the time. If you do not know and understand it, you will be defeated in your dreamland and wonder why.

In our foundational scripture, which is under the old covenant, God instructs, *"And you shall offer (or sacrifice) on that day...a male lamb of the first year, without blemish...."* This is a type of Christ. In the New Testament, John the Baptist said, *"...Behold! The Lamb of God that taketh away the sin of the world!"* (John 1:29, KJV). Jesus was a lamb without spot or wrinkle. The parallels of these passages prove that this is a matter of covenant. It has nothing to do with whether it is Old or New Testament. God wants you to understand that obedience to Him in this area is about your covenant responsibility. Leviticus 23:14 says: **"It shall be a statute forever throughout your generations in all your dwellings."**

With this statement, the Bible settles the fact that this is not exclusive to the old covenant. I need to establish this. If the Bible says, *"it shall be a statute forever,"* this means it is still pertinent to life today – no matter when today may be. It did not end with the old covenant, and God could not be any clearer about this. It shall be a principle to be observed and obeyed. This is not the law of Moses. This is a principle of covenant. He said, *"It shall be a statute forever throughout your generations in all your dwellings."*

> *"It shall be a statute forever,"* means the principles are not exclusive to old or new covenant. They are still pertinent to life today – no matter when today may be.

Many differentiate between old and new covenant instructions. In the case of the Firstfruit, however, it is an old covenant principle that the new covenant gives us greater liberty to fulfill. It is very important to understand this concept of liberty. To fully comprehend it, you must understand that new covenant principles do not release us from old covenant principles. God is still God. He still wants what He wants. He still does what He says. If He says to do something, our calling it "old covenant" does not release us from the responsibility of performing that act of obedience. What the new covenant does is release us into greater liberty, or provide more avenues and resources to act out the will of God. Here is an example. Leviticus 25:8-11 reads:

> The New Covenant does not negate the Old Covenant. It gives us greater liberty to fulfill the principles of the Old Covenant.

> *And you shall count seven sabbaths of years for yourself, seven times seven years; and the time of the seven sabbaths of years shall be to you forty nine years. Then you shall cause the trumpet of the Jubilee to sound on the tenth day of the seventh month; on the Day of Atonement you shall make the trumpet to sound throughout all your land...**and proclaim liberty** throughout all the land to all its inhabitants. It shall be*

> *a Jubilee for you; and each of you shall return to his possession, and each of you shall return to his family. That fiftieth year shall be a Jubilee to you...*

What this old covenant scripture is saying is that the year of Jubilee could only come at a specific time – every 50 years. Now let us compare this to a new covenant passage, Luke 4:18-19.

> *The Spirit of the Lord is upon Me, because He has anointed Me To preach the gospel to the poor; He has sent Me to heal the brokenhearted,* **to proclaim liberty** *to the captives, and recovery of sight to the blind, to set at liberty those who are oppressed; to proclaim the acceptable year of the Lord.*

Both refer to the "acceptable year of the Lord." The difference is that in the new covenant, it did not have to be at a certain time. Greater liberty is granted whenever you proclaim it! I want you to understand this because I want you to be educated. But you must read the Bible for yourself and not allow anyone to talk you out of the truth that God reveals in His word.

THE AUTHORITY OF THREE

Part of understanding the truth that will move you into your dream dimension has to do with understanding the authority governing your life. The Bible articulates that God establishes divine authority in threes. The Godhead is three: Father, Son and Holy Spirit. God created three lights to rule the heavens: the sun, the moon and the stars. The plan of redemption falls out in threes: death, burial and resurrection. The old covenant tabernacle had three dimensions: the outer court, the inner court and the Holy of Holies. God created man as three parts: spirit, soul and body. In the natural realm, our government has three branches:

> God establishes divine authority in threes. When one of the three governing areas is out of place, the result is chaos, disorder and darkness.

executive, judicial and legislative. Heaven itself was orchestrated under the authority of three archangels: Michael, Gabriel and Lucifer. When one of the three areas is out of order (as in the fall of Lucifer), chaos, disorder and darkness result. All three elements must be in place if you are going to have order and function.

In the financial area of your life, three divine principles must be in place to ensure order and prosperity for the believer. For years the church has only taught two of these principles: the tithe and the offering. Because this third dimension — the Firstfruit — has been missing, the church today has been breaking even, but not prospering. Even though this area of financial covenant is outlined in your Bible, this may be the first time the principle of Firstfruits giving has been illuminated for you in this way. God says it is time for you to gain the missing key needed to unlock your prosperity. I am tired of seeing the people of God do all they know how to do and still only break even. The Firstfruit is key to order and authority in the financial realm. Putting these principles into effect in your life will bring order and facilitate prosperity in your finances.

Allow me to turn your attention to Leviticus 27. I want you to see that each of these elements must be put in place and all three of them are what the Bible calls **devoted, accursed, or things doomed to destruction**. In Leviticus 27:26 the Bible declares, *"But the firstborn of the animal, which should be the Lord's firstborn, no man shall dedicate; whether it is an ox or sheep, it is the Lord's."* The Bible says, *"It is the Lord's,"* meaning it is devoted, consecrated or set apart. In other words, God says it already belongs to Him. He goes on to say concerning the Firstfruit, *"no man shall dedicate it."* You cannot devote (or dedicate) it as something else because God says it is already devoted to Him, and God's word is the first and final authority.

He declares that the Firstfruit is a devoted offering. When the Bible says that you cannot dedicate it as something else, this means the Lord will not allow you to mix or replace the Firstfruit with the tithe or the offering and receive a blessing of increase. If you do so, you will have taken one of the three out of its proper place.

The Bible also says that the offering, which the Lord asks for, is a devoted thing. Leviticus 27:27-28 states:

And if it is an unclean animal, then he shall redeem it according to your valuation, and shall add one-fifth to it; or if it is not redeemed, then it shall be sold according to your valuation. Nevertheless no devoted offering that a man may devote to the Lord of all that he has, both man and beast, or the field of his possession, shall be sold or redeemed; ***every devoted offering is most holy to the Lord.***

Concerning your offerings, there is a distinction between a devoted offering and an offering you determine in your heart to give. I want to separate the two because you need to understand the difference. There is the offering that you decide to give out of the goodness of your heart because you have such a love for God and an appreciation for Him that you determine, "I just want to give this to God." This type offering is not a devoted offering because God did not ask for it.

A freewill offering – or "devoted offering" as in the above scripture – is not one in which you decide to bring God whatever you want. A freewill offering is when God specifically asks you to bring Him a gift, and of your own freewill, you bring Him exactly what He wants. You must understand that when it comes to the offerings, God designates certain types to bring. When the Lord says, "I want you to bring me this," and you determine in your heart to obey, your offering becomes devoted. Imagine that God impresses upon you to give a $100 offering. If you decide to do it, it is a freewill offering, and is devoted to the Lord as such. It cannot be called the Firstfruit or the tithe. You must be careful

> A freewill offering is one in which God tells you what He wants you to give and you agree to do it.

not to fail in keeping your promises to God concerning the offerings. The moment He asks you for an offering and you agree to give it, that offering is devoted. If you keep it, it brings a curse. This is why the Bible says it is *"Better not to vow than to vow and not pay. Do not let your mouth cause your flesh to sin..."* (Ecclesiastes 5:5-6) This means that we are not to be quick to pledge an offering if we have not heard from God to do so. When we make a vow and do not pay, it is a sin of the flesh. You have sinned because the money you promised to pay belongs to God. Keeping it brings a curse that blocks your increase.

Continuing in Leviticus 27:30, 32:

And all the tithe of the land, whether of the seed of the land or of the fruit of the tree, is the Lord's. It is holy to the Lord...And concerning the tithe of the herd or the flock, or whatever passes under the rod, the tenth one shall be holy to the Lord.

Here the Bible clearly shows us that the tithe is not the first tenth, it is simply a tenth. Consider it this way: If I have ten $100 bills and I offer to give you one of them, it does not matter which one I give you. All of them are worth the same amount. It says in the scripture that the tenth one is the Lord's. Therefore, the tithe and the Firstfruit are different things. Notice verse 30 says, *"And all the tithe..."* This means that the tithe and the devoted offerings are separate from one another. Remember, there are three different things the Bible calls devoted or consecrated to the Lord: the Firstfruit, the tithe, and the offering.

Understanding this distinction and exercising these instructions will elevate you into the dimension of increase and obedience that will cause you to be blessed on every hand! Before you can put this into place, however, some of you will recognize that there are things you need to reconcile with God, and you need to do it immediately. There is no need to be under condemnation or be afraid. Simply receive God's word, begin to do what He declares and watch God bless you on a new level.

THIS IS A COVENANT MATTER

I want to call your attention to the law of devoted things in Joshua 6:17-18. Remember that this particular passage of scripture talks about the battle of Jericho, Israel's first victory in the land of promise. The Word of God reads, *"Now the city shall be doomed by the Lord to destruction"... "And you,* **by all means, abstain from the accursed things***, lest you become accursed when you take of the accursed things..."*

Keep in mind that "doomed to destruction" and "accursed" are interchangeable. In other words, God says, whatever you have to do to abstain from taking of the accursed thing, do it. The principle is: If you take or hold on to what is doomed to destruction or accursed, then you become doomed to destruction and accursed. Look again at verse 18, focusing on the latter part: *"and make the camp of Israel a curse, and trouble it."*

This divine principle is illustrated in the story when the children of Israel were defeated by Ai – a small, insignificant opponent – because Achan took of the accursed things. Jericho, the battle before Ai, was the first battle fought by the children of Israel. Because it was their first battle in their dreamland, it was a Firstfruit to God and all the spoils from the battle were not to be taken, but offered to the Lord. However, Achan took of the spoils (which were accursed) and released a curse over the entire camp. When they fought against Ai, they were defeated because the Firstfruit was not rendered to the Lord and their victory was blocked. Joshua could not figure out why they had been beaten by an opponent who should have been defeated easily, so he went to the Lord in prayer seeking an answer. In Joshua 7:10-12, the Lord replies:

> God says, "By all means, abstain from the accursed thing."

> *...Get up! Why do you lie thus on your face? Israel has sinned, and they have also transgressed My covenant which I commanded them. For they have even taken some of the accursed things, and have both stolen and*

deceived; and they have also put it among their own stuff. Therefore the children of Israel could not stand before their enemies, but turned their backs before their enemies because they have become doomed to destruction...

Notice the last part: *"...they have become doomed to destruction..."* This is why you cannot stand against your enemies. When you take of the accursed thing, which is doomed to destruction, you become doomed to destruction because you have it in your possession. This is not the devil defeating you. This is not your enemy defeating you. **This is the word of the Lord defeating you.** It is resting on your head because God says that when you take of the things that are devoted to destruction, you become devoted to destruction; and therefore, you cannot stand against your enemies.

Because of this truth, it is vitally important that you and I find out what is devoted to destruction and remove it from our house and our possession.

> The enemy is not defeating you in your finances; the Word of God is defeating you.

Concerning the accursed things or the things devoted to destruction, notice what the Lord says when Israel takes of it. He says, *"Israel has sinned, and they have also transgressed My covenant, which I commanded them. For they have even taken of the accursed things..."* I want you to get this because as I read this one day the Spirit of the Lord said to me, "Son, do not miss what I said. *'Israel has sinned **and** they have also transgressed My covenant.'"* God says those are two different things.

This is not just a matter of sin. God says, "I can deal with your sin. I can handle you missing the mark. I can deal with your imperfection. You are not going to be perfect. You are going to slip. But by all means, **do not break covenant!**" God wants you to understand that He knows you are never going to be flawless; but as long as your covenant is intact, He can bless you over your transgression. However, when you break covenant with Him, there is nothing He can do for you.

I told my staff, "Listen, there will always be problems. There will always be attitudes and opinions and things that do not get done. There will always be disagreements. There will always be power struggles. God understands that. But as long as we keep covenant, He will fight for us. On the other hand, if you are falling short and breaking covenant, there is no help for you." I said to them, "I would rather have an alcoholic on my staff than a non-tither because God can deal with an alcoholic." He can handle an addiction, but if covenant is broken, there is no **power** to deal with the addiction.

It is a covenant matter. You need to understand this, child of God. This is not about money. This is about covenant. God said Israel sinned and transgressed His covenant. The reason God has not supplied your need is not because you slept with your ex two weeks ago; it is not because you threw four-letter words at your boss last week. Let us be real because this is one way the devil tries to defeat you. Do not get me wrong, it is not a good thing for you to sin, but God knows that you are not going to be perfect. The reason you are not getting your need met is because you sinned and you broke covenant with God. He says, "I can handle sin. I do not want you to commit sin, but I can handle that. But if you continue to break covenant with Me, there is no power to supply correction for the matter."

INVOKE GOD'S POWER WITH THE TITHE

The blessing of the tithe is not a money blessing; it is a power blessing. It is a blessing that releases the power of God in your life. That is why you do not increase by tithing. Some of

The Five Power Blessings of the Tithe
1) Revelation and insight
2) Trans-generational blessing
3) Protection
4) Divinely regulated harvest
5) Endowment to prosper

you are faithful in your tithing, but you are not increasing. You are getting your need met. You are breaking even. God comes through, but usually it is not exactly when you feel you need Him.

You see, we say, "He may not come when you want Him to, but He is always on time." Child of God, there is a place you can get to in your finances where He is there before you. The Bible says *"...For your Father knows the things you have need of before you ask Him"* (Matthew 6:8). Despite this truth, we are content to praise Him with, "He may not come when you want Him..." Forget that foolishness. I want Him there before I get in trouble. I want God to call me and tell me where to pick up my blessing. I see in the Word that there is a way to get there – by obedience.

Regarding the blessing of the tithe, Malachi 3:10 instructs: *"Bring all the tithes into the storehouse, that there may be food in My house, and try Me now in this... if I will not open for you the windows of heaven and pour out for you such blessing that there will not be room enough to receive it."* Again, the "open windows of heaven" is not a money blessing. It is not a material blessing. I have been tithing all of my adult life and even in my childhood. I have never received a package dropped out of heaven, never received money from the sky. I have never seen a car fall into my driveway that came from heaven. So then, what is the blessing of the "open window?"

God asked me years ago, "Son, what do you do through a window?" I said, "God, you look through it." He said, "That is what the blessing of the tithe brings." **The first power blessing of the tithe brings revelation**. It is a blessing of supernatural vision and insight. Then He told me, "If I open the windows of heaven, I am allowing you to see what things are like up here. This lets you know what it should be like down there."

In Genesis 14 Abram tithed to Melchizedek. The first verse of the next chapter opens with these words, *"After these things the word of the Lord came to Abram in a vision, saying, '...I am your shield, your exceedingly great reward'"* (Genesis 15:1). What "things" is God talking about? He is talking about Abram obeying God and **tithing** to Melchizedek. In other words, once he tithed,

God gave him vision into his promise. God gave Abram the power to be able to see what God wanted, what He purposed to do, where He desired to lead and direct him.

The second power blessing of the tithe returns a transgenerational blessing. Again, this is practical teaching. If God gives you a blessing that there is not room enough for you to receive then you do not get that blessing. Hebrews 7:1-6 tells us how this is possible:

> *For this Melchizedek, King of Salem, priest of the Most High God... to whom also Abraham gave a tenth part of all, first being translated "king of righteousness," and then also king of Salem, meaning "king of peace," without father, without mother, without genealogy, having neither beginning of days nor end of life, but made like the Son of God, remains a priest continually. Now consider how great this man was [meaning Melchizedek], to whom even the patriarch Abraham gave a tenth of the spoils. And indeed those who are of the sons of Levi, who receive the priesthood, have a commandment to receive tithes from the people according to the law, that is, from their brethren, though they have come from the loins of Abraham; but he whose genealogy is not derived from them received tithes from Abraham and blessed him who had the promises.*

This is the blessing God speaks of when He says, *"not room enough to receive."* Levi is four generations down from Abram. Abram begot Isaac. Isaac begot Jacob; Jacob begot 12 sons, who are known as the sons of Israel or the heads of the tribes, of which Levi is one of them. I want you to see that Levi is Abraham's great, great, grandson; and the Bible says that Levi is qualified to become a priest and is placed in the priesthood to the position where he receives sustenance because he was in Abram's loins when Abram met Melchizedek.

Your life is not long enough to get the full blessing of tithing. When you tithe, God sets up your children's children's children so they will not have to start from ground zero. Your tithe reaps a power blessing that transcends throughout your generations.

The third power blessing of the tithe is protection. Malachi 3:11 reads: *"I will rebuke the devourer for your sakes."* The rebuking of the devourer is God defending your possessions. Again, this is not money, it is power. It is God keeping away the enemy that would seek to steal your blessing.

The same verse then moves us into **the fourth blessing, which is divinely regulated harvest**. It continues with, *"neither shall your vine cast her fruit before the time in the field"* (KJV). When you tithe, God gets involved in your cycle of receiving so that, as you honor Him, He makes sure that whatever is supposed to come to you drops off the tree at the right time. It will not come early. It will not come late. No one else will be able to get it. It will be released when you get there.

The fifth power blessing of the tithe is an endowment to prosper. God says, *"And all nations will call you blessed"* (Malachi 3:12). In other words, your color or nationality will not matter because this will work for you. It does not matter which ethnic group looks at you, they will declare that you are a person empowered to prosper. That is the meaning of "blessed" – empowered to prosper. They will say, "I don't know about her. All I know is whatever she does keeps working. She always has enough. I never see her struggling."

REPLENISHMENT AND EXCHANGE

The offering allows you to reap a blessing of replenishment and exchange. It does not move you into increase. You do not even need your Bible to comprehend that. Some of you are tithing and giving offerings but you are not increasing, you are simply getting back to even.

In Proverbs 3:9 where it says, *"Honour the Lord with thy substance, and with the firstfruits of all thine increase"* (KJV), that has nothing to do with your tithe. Even though we have applied this scripture to tithe in the church for years, it has nothing to do with tithing because the tithe is not **your** substance. You cannot honor the Lord by bringing Him what already belongs to Him. The tithe is His substance. The offering comes from your substance.

Jesus says in Luke 6:38, *"Give, and it will be given to you: good measure, pressed down, shaken together, and running over will be put unto your bosom."* It is clear that when God says "give," He is not talking about the tithe because that devoted thing already belongs to Him. The only thing you can do is **bring** the tithe to Him. That is why God does not say, "Give all the tithe." He says, "Bring all the tithe..." This scripture in Luke 6 refers to two types of offerings. There is the offering that is the Lord's because He asks you to give it. Then there is the Firstfruit.

Jesus says that when you give, the first thing that will happen from your giving is you will begin to receive good measure. In other words, the measure that you give will be the same measure you receive, and it will be good. "Pressed down and shaken together" means that God will change the form of your offering. He says, "I change it in form and it comes back to you in the form of favor. You bring me an offering, I change its form and it comes back to you in the form of healing or deliverance from an addiction." You cannot buy those things. The only way to get them is to exchange what you have in order to initiate God's involvement and change its form so it returns as you need it.

Now get this. God says, "You bring Me an offering and when I shake it together and give it back to you, it will be in the form of debt cancellation." But understand that cancellation of debt is not increase. It is catching you back up to zero. It is a great blessing – don't get me wrong. We shout about it and thank God for it, but **that is not increase!** When God cancels your debt, He only gets you back to even.

Healing gets you back to even. Healing is not increase. Thank God for the miracle of healing, but it is not increase. Healing means there was something out of order in your body and not functioning in the way God created it to work. When God heals you, He puts your body back into the condition it should have always been.

God does not want you to break even. He wants you to increase. Jesus wants you to have the kind of body that can perform supernaturally with an "S" on your chest! You last longer. You go farther. You pray harder.

> God does not want you to merely break even. He wants you to increase!

How to Increase

In order to prepare for your blessing you must realize this fact: God is going to increase you massively, and He is going to increase you quickly. What God desires to get into your hands is not going to take a long time if you and I will simply obey Him. God has purposed to bring each of us into dominion in our dreams, whatever they are. You are not supposed to be just another person doing what you are doing – you are supposed to be the one with dominion in that area. You are supposed to be the trendsetter, the trailblazer, the one whom other people look to. That is what it means to be the head and not the tail. It means you are ahead of the curve, ahead of the trend. The Holy Ghost has shown you what is to come before it happens. You are already prepared for it. He has positioned you to bring you into dominion. He specifically told me to get this message across to His people. "I want you to make sure," He said, "that the people not only understand this, but that their faith is alive as they move in their understanding of it."

> God will show you His purpose for your life before it happens.

To obtain this dominion, you must understand that you need all three components of your financial covenant working for you. We have discussed the tithe and the offering. Now, let us discuss the key to increase - the Firstfruit.

I recall Israel's deliverance from Egypt in the book of Exodus. It was after Pharaoh played "Let's Make a Deal" with the children of Israel and told them they could leave, but not take their flocks and herds. Despite this command from Pharaoh, Moses said: *"Our livestock also shall go with us; not a hoof shall be left behind. For we must take some of them to serve the Lord our God"* (Exodus 10:26). He was not willing to leave any material or any of their financial wealth and prosperity. Their actual deliverance, however, came when God reached down and took the Firstfruit of Egypt.

Exodus 11:4-8 reads:

Thus says the Lord: "About midnight I will go out into the midst of Egypt; and all the firstborn in the land of Egypt shall die, from the firstborn of Pharaoh who sits on his throne, even to the firstborn of the female servant who is behind the handmill, and all the firstborn of the animals. Then there shall be a great cry throughout all the land of Egypt, such as was not like it before, nor shall be like it again. But against none of the children of Israel shall a dog move its tongue, against man or beast, that you may know that the Lord does make a difference between the Egyptians and Israel."

At first, this puzzled me. I had to ask God why He took the firstborn of Egypt and not Israel. What He revealed to me could not be more poignant concerning our subject. Egypt had the wealth of Israel. The Egyptians thought it was their wealth, but God's people had actually built it for them. They had Israel's property. That is why God did not take the firstborn of Israel, but the firstborn of Egypt.

Remember I said it does not take God long to respond. When the Firstfruit was taken from Egypt, the deliverance became effective the very next day! Sons and daughters were being set

> It does not take God long to respond.

free. Cattle started being loosed. Silver and gold started coming into the hands of God's people.

Over the years, I have learned that God's people are destroyed for lack of knowledge. Sometimes, they are not even destroyed for lack of obedience. They are destroyed for lack of knowing what they should receive for their obedience. If you obey and you do not know what you should get for it, then you cannot contend for it, you cannot fight for it, you cannot command it. God said, *"Ask me of things to come concerning my sons, and concerning the works of my hands command ye me"* (Isaiah 45:11, KJV). In other words, "If I said it, tell me, and I will stand by My word." But you cannot put Him in remembrance of His word if you do not know what His word says. Child of God, your days of living with a lack of knowledge are over!

> Often times, we are not destroyed due to lack of obedience. We are destroyed for lack of knowledge of what our obedience should produce.

As we get into the specific blessings associated with Firstfruit giving, it is imperative that you first believe that God wants you blessed! The prosperity covenant God has given to you and me – the blessing of increase that God has promised – is only going to work if you first believe that God wants you blessed. Many of you are tired of obeying God and not seeing His blessing on your life as it is in scripture. I would like to continue from our foundational scripture, Leviticus 23. Let us look at verses 10 and 11.

> God wants you blessed!

Speak to the children of Israel, and say to them: "When you come into the land which I give to you, and reap its harvest, then you shall bring a sheaf of the firstfruits of your harvest to the priest. He shall wave the sheaf before the Lord, to be accepted on your behalf; on the day after the Sabbath, the priest shall wave it."

I want you to notice that God says the priest shall wave it. And when he waves your offering in presentation to God, it will be accepted on your behalf. In other words, you cannot do this for yourself. In order to activate the blessings associated with the Firstfruit, it must be given to the priest. Your priest is God's representative on earth and it is important to honor those whom God sends to you. Jesus said in Matthew 10:40: *"He who receives Me receives Him who sent Me."* Some people mistakenly think they can serve God without connecting their service to a man of God, and that is why many of you go to church but have no blessing, no anointing, and no glory on your houses. If you do not receive those whom God sends, you do not receive God. Now that you know how to activate your Firstfruit offering, let us look at the blessing principles associated with this offering.

Blessing Principle #1: The Firstfruit is the singular part of your financial and material covenant that brings increase.

This is why you must do all three. As discussed earlier in this chapter, there is a specific blessing attached to each element of your financial covenant. The one attached to the tithe is a power blessing. As you tithe, God speaks to you. He releases the power for you to get wealth. The only problem is, you recognize where the wealth is supposed to come from, but you never get it! You have not increased because you did not know about the Firstfruit offering and that you were supposed to be applying it as a facet of your giving.

Remember, all three financial components – Firstfruit, tithe and offering – work in concert. You must do all three in order to get the full blessing of your covenant. In addition, you cannot take from one and give to another. Now, if you do not want the full blessing, I cannot help you; but for those of you who want what God has for you, you must know that the blessing comes by performing all three acts of obedience. Then, when your pastor does his part – waving your offering before God, calling your name out before Him and commanding a blessing of increase on your house – there is no way a blessing can avoid you! You have obeyed. Your pastor has obeyed. God must respond.

In other words, God says that when you honor Him with your substance (the offering, not the tithe), and bring Him the Firstfruit of all your increase, "your barns will be filled with plenty, and your vats will overflow with new wine" (Proverbs 3:10). When your barns are filled with plenty, you will need some new barns, and if you do not have the blessing of increase, you will not be able to get new barns.

I want to give one more reference to support this teaching. Let us examine 2 Kings 4:38-41:

And Elisha returned to Gilgal, and there was a famine in the land. Now the sons of the prophets were sitting before him; and he said to his servant, "Put on the large pot, and boil stew for the sons of the prophets." So, one went out into the field to gather herbs, and found a wild vine, and gathered from it a lap full of wild gourds, and came and sliced them into the pot of stew, though they did not know what they were. Then they served it to the men to eat. Now it happened, as they were eating the stew, that they cried out and said, "Man of God, there is death in the pot!" And they could not eat it. So he said, "Then bring some flour." And he put it into the pot, and said, "Serve it to the people, that they may eat." And there was nothing harmful in the pot.

There is a problem. There is death in the pot, so the pot needs healing. The man of God requests flour (this is an offering). The people obeyed. Now watch what happens. When they bring the flour and he puts it in the pot, it is healed. The death leaves the pot, but remember, healing is just a blessing of exchange. Let us continue to verses 42-44.

Then a man came from Baal Shalisha, and brought the man of God bread of the firstfruits, twenty loaves of barley bread, and newly ripened grain in his knapsack. And he said, "Give it to the people, that they may eat."

But his servants said, "What? Shall I set this before one hundred men?" He said again, "Give it to the people, that they may eat; for thus says the Lord: 'They shall eat and have some left over.'" So he set it before them; and they ate and had some left over, according to the word of the Lord.

When the man from Baal Shalisha placed his Firstfruit into the hands of a man of God it brought increase. The increase was so large that everyone ate **"and had some left over."** This is how our God operates. He not only wants to bless you, He wants to bless you abundantly!

Blessing Principle #2: The giving of the Firstfruit is the act of financial obedience that sanctifies or separates your whole material and financial possession from the kingdom of darkness.

Now again, the Firstfruit, tithe, and offering are all acts of financial obedience. They are all acts of your covenant with God. But the Firstfruit is the act of financial obedience that sanctifies or separates your whole material and financial possession, or lump, from the kingdom of darkness. The tithe does not separate your lump. The tithe gives you creativity. It gives you vision. It gives you insight and connection to resources.

Do you remember when God was making covenant with Abram? The Bible says in Genesis 15 that Abram fell asleep and when he woke up, he had to get a stick and beat the fowls of the air off his sacrifice. This is a picture of what the enemy tries to do. The devouring spirits want access to what you offer up to God, and they want access to the rest of what you have. They want access to your covenant. God says the Firstfruit offering is how you snatch everything in your financial and material life out of the hands of the enemy.

What you have to do is to remove your stuff out from under the devil's dominion. You have to take your entire financial and material life out of his kingdom, and God says this is the way to do it. I do not know about you, but I want the devil out of all my stuff. I am tired of God's people obeying and praying and fasting and believing and standing and coming to church and reading the Bible and confessing the Word and the devil still has access to their stuff! He is trying to rob you as quickly as you can bring it in. I am tired of it. I want the devil out of my stuff and I want him out of yours!

Romans 11:16 says, *"For if the firstfruit is holy, the lump is also holy; and if the root is holy, so are the branches."* Here is what this means: if the Firstfruit is holy, meaning sanctified or separated, then the rest of your possessions will also be considered holy unto God.

In other words, He says that if you will do what He tells us to do with the Firstfruit and put it into the hands of your priest, who is your representative of God, He will rebuke the enemy off of your possessions. You see, a lot of people will not do this because they never get to the place where they see their man of God as God's representative to them. That is one of the reasons they argue about lavishing the man of God with blessing. "Why should I give to him? Why should he have that?" Why? Because when you give to a holy man of God who carries an anointing of God, God reckons it as being given to Him. He reckons it as worship to Him.

When the Firstfruit is put into the hands of the priest, God, in essence says, "I have the Firstfruit in my hand. Therefore, all of it is in My hands." Conversely, if the Firstfruit is kept in your power, the rest of it is in your power and is subjected to the system of this world, which is under the dominion of the enemy.

Look at Luke 4:5-7. This is the account of Jesus being tempted in the wilderness after He has been anointed by the Spirit of God. It says,

> *Then the devil, taking Him up on a high mountain, showed Him all the kingdoms [or the dominions] of the world in a moment of time. And the devil said to Him, "All this authority I will give You, and their glory; for this has been delivered to me, and I give it to whomever I wish.*

Here, glory is the Greek word *doxa*. It means wealth. It means to be heavily weighted down with good. Throughout the scripture, glory has the connotation of material wealth and blessing.

The Bible says that Satan showed Jesus the kingdoms of the world. That does not mean he showed Him governments and thrones. This is a spiritual concept. Jesus is in the wilderness – this is happening in the spirit. The devil is showing Him the structures and domains of the kingdoms of this world: the economic kingdom, the political kingdom, the educational kingdom, the structures, the rulers, the principalities, regional princes, and demonic and territorial devils that rule and govern this world system.

He has basically told Jesus, "I'm running this world's economic system. I stole it from Adam in the garden. Now I'm running it, and I give it to who I want to have it." That is why the most wicked, perverse people are the ones who have the devil's wealth. It is because they are the ones who will continue to fund his kingdom and his objectives. The devil wants to get his stuff into the hands of people who will advance his cause, and God wants to get His wealth into the hands of people who will advance His cause. My Bible says, *"The earth is the Lord's, and all its fullness"* (Psalm 24:1). In Haggai 2:8, God said, *"The silver is Mine, and the gold is Mine."* The world's wealth is supposed to be in the hands of God's people. The wealth of the music industry is not supposed to belong to adulterers and fornicators. This is the Word of God! I cannot make you believe this; God's word gives all the evidence you need. Once you understand what you can expect God to do for you when you work your covenant, you will not want to live any other way!

In order for God to prosper His people, He had to determine a way to separate your possessions from Satan's dominion. It is called the Firstfruit. When you take the Firstfruit to God, He takes the rest of your possession out of Satan's dominion. He tells the devils that they cannot touch it. Then when your priest on earth tells the devils on earth they cannot touch it and speak blessing and increase on your life, that agreement commands you to prosper.

Blessing Principle #3: The Firstfruit causes a blessing to rest on your house.

Understanding what a blessing is should cause you to shout! A blessing, or an endowment to prosper, is something that is given freely with no strings attached. Another word for endowment is "gift." A blessing is a gift!

Where does God say a blessing will rest on your house just because of your obedience? Look at Ezekiel 44:30. *"The best of all firstfruits of any kind, and every sacrifice of any kind from all your sacrifices, shall be the priest's; also you shall give to the priest the first of your ground meal, to cause a blessing to rest on your house."*

> Your obedience causes a blessing to rest on your house!

When you put this into effect, you get a blessing that causes a gift of prosperity to move to your address. In other words, when you do this and God does what He promised to do, a blessing – literally an angel, a spirit of prosperity – rests on your house.

It will be there when you wake up, there when you brush your teeth, there when you eat dinner, and there when you go to sleep. This also means the blessing comes on anyone who comes into your house. You cannot live in my house and not be touched by this endowment, this gift that God has placed on my house.

This is serious! A blessing on your house means that it stays there no matter who comes and goes. You will have the authority to say, "No, no, no – you cannot be a crack addict in this house. You cannot stay on drugs, not in my house. Not because I will kick you out, but because you cannot stay that way and live here!"

These principles are what will bring you dominion in your dream dimension. God wants to bring new blessings into your life. You will no longer break even – you will increase! You will increase because that is God's will and purpose for your life, and it will happen through your obedience.

****

Father, we thank You for Your Word. Regardless of what it looks like today, we still believe Your Word. Now, make us doers and not hearers only. We rejoice in the revelation, but we will rejoice even greater in the manifestation of our blessing as we are obedient and move toward fulfilling Your purpose for our lives. In the name of Jesus, I bless your people now. I pray, oh God, that those who read these words of instruction will get all three of these covenant principles working in their financial life. I pray, Father, in the name of Jesus, that every demon and devil of darkness and lack will be ejected from their atmosphere because your people are obeying your Word. May all the angels of increase and blessing and prosperity go with them every day. God prosper these people. Let the blessing rest on their houses, not just for them, but also for their families. Let them feel something different in the house. I thank You, Lord, that their lives are changing now as they believe and obey. In Jesus' name. Amen.

CHAPTER V

CHRIST: THE FIRSTFRUIT

We have outlined the principles governing Firstfruit giving. Now we will see how God put these principles to work to produce the resurrection of Christ, who is the Firstfruit. The entire resurrection of Christ is based on the principle of Firstfruits offering. If Christ is the Firstfruit, then He must have first been an offering. 1 Peter 2:24 tells us that Christ was made an offering for our sins: *"who Himself **bore our sins** in His own body on the tree, that we, having died to sins, might live for righteousness— by whose stripes you were healed."* Isaiah 53:10 gives us the familiar redemptive passage: *"Yet it pleased the Lord to bruise Him; He has put Him to grief. When You make His **soul** an offering for sin."* The Bible says God, the Father, gave an offering to Himself when He made Jesus' soul an offering for our sin.

1 Corinthians 15:20 declares, *"...Christ is risen from the dead, and has become the Firstfruits of those who have fallen asleep."* It does not say Jesus was the first one resurrected. It says He was the Firstfruit. Lazarus, Nain's son and Jairus' daughter were all resurrected before Jesus. So, do not confuse the Firstfruit with the first one. Christ was not the first one risen from the dead, but he was the Firstfruit. The Firstfruit is not simply the first one. The thing that makes it the Firstfruit is what you *do* with it.

Man is spirit, soul and body. Jesus' soul and body became an offering for man's sin and were sacrificed for it: *"All we like sheep have gone astray; We have turned, every one, to his own way; And the Lord has laid on Him the iniquity of us all"*(Isaiah 53:6). From the cross, Jesus put the Firstfruit—His spirit—into the hands of the Priest who is the Father.

*Now it was about the sixth hour, and there was darkness over all the earth until the ninth hour. Then the sun was darkened, and the veil of the temple was torn in two. And when Jesus had cried out with a loud voice, He said, "Father **into Your hands I commit My spirit**"* (Luke 23:44-46).

Because Jesus committed His spirit to God, our spirits are also holy unto the Father. *"For if the firstfruit is holy, the lump is also holy; and if the root is holy, so are the branches"* (Romans 11:16). Once Jesus commits His spirit into the hands of the Father, it is impossible for the devil to hold His soul or His body! Once you put your Firstfruit in the hands of the priest, it is impossible for the devil to hold onto your household. It does not matter whether or not you are in debt. It does not matter whether or not the IRS is after you. Your possessions are separated from the devil and it makes no difference whether or not the devil tries to hold them.

After the resurrection, Peter preaches that the resurrection was an act designed by the Father to put the Firstfruit—Jesus—in the hands of the Priest:

Men of Israel, hear these words: Jesus of Nazareth, a Man attested by God to you by miracles, wonders, and signs which God did through Him in your midst, as you yourselves also know—Him, **being delivered by the determined purpose and foreknowledge of God**, *you have taken by lawless hands, have crucified, and put to death;* **whom God raised up, having loosed the pains of death, because it was not possible that He should be held by it** (Acts 2:22 - 24).

Once that happened, the resurrection of the soul and body was inevitable. In 1 Peter 3, the Bible teaches that Jesus went into the lower regions of the earth to preach to the spirits in prison. It was at that time, when Jesus became sin, that the devil said, "We have

Him now." Understand what is happening at this point. Jesus is separated from the Father, His body has become sin and His soul is being made an offering for sin. Death and hell put their hands on Him and said, "We have you now, Son of God." Then a Voice came and said, *"O Death, where is your sting? O Hades, where is your victory?"* (1 Corinthians 15:55). God commanded the devil to loose His Son because Jesus put the Firstfruit in His Father's hand. This assured Jesus of a resurrection, but not us. When Jesus put His spirit into the hands of the Father, He was the Firstfruit that assured His lump - soul and body - would be resurrected.

Jesus went down into the lower parts of the earth and after three days, His spirit returned to the body that lay in the grave. 1 Corinthians 15:35-38 tells us how a resurrection occurs and how things are raised up:

> *But someone will say, 'How are the dead raised up? And with what body do they come?' Foolish one, what you sow is not made alive unless it dies. And what you sow, you do not sow that body that shall be, but mere grain – perhaps wheat or some other* **grain***. But God gives it a body as He pleases, and to each seed its own body.*

Paul describes how after you sow a seed and it dies, the body that returns to you is new – a different thing. When you sow an apple seed, the seed is the body that goes into the ground. But when it returns—is resurrected—it is no longer a seed. It is a tree.

So it is with the resurrection of the dead. The body is sown in corruption, meaning subject to death. It is raised in incorruption, meaning power over death. It is sown in dishonor; it is raised in glory. It is sown in weakness; it is raised in power. It is sown a natural body; it is raised a spiritual body. There is a natural and a spiritual body. The natural body of Jesus having become sin was sown in corruption, dishonor and weakness: But, the spiritual body was raised in incorruption, glory and power.

On the resurrection side of His empty grave, Jesus, whose *"visage was marred more than any man,"* is perfectly intact (Isaiah 52:14). He rises, goes to the garden, and a woman from whom He cast out seven devils, Mary Magdalene, comes to the tomb. The Bible says that when she enters the garden on her way to the tomb, she walked right by Him, thinking He was a gardener:

> *Now when she had said this, she turned around and **saw** Jesus standing there, and did not know that it was Jesus. Jesus said to her, "Woman, why are you weeping? Whom are you seeking?" She, supposing Him to be the gardener, said to Him, "Sir, if you have carried Him away, tell me where you have laid Him, and I will take Him away"* (John 20: 14-15).

Mary Magdalene saw Jesus crucified. She thought that if she was going to see Him raised, He should still look bruised and cut. That was not the case. He did not look that way because God gave Him another body; a spiritual body raised in power, glory, and with dominion over death.

When Mary Magdalene walks by Jesus and He asks her, "Why are you weeping?" she replies that she weeps because her Master has been taken. She goes on to tell this man she believes to be the gardener that she is searching for Jesus and asks if He knows where Jesus was taken. Jesus calls to her as if to say, "It's Me, Mary!" (John 20:16). Continuing in the same verse, Mary looks at Him and says, "*Rabboni*! (which is to say, Teacher)." In verse 17, Jesus says to her, *"Do not cling to Me, for I have not yet ascended to My Father."*

John 20:26-27 confirms Jesus is now in a spiritual body, different than before the crucifixion, because He walks through closed doors.

> *And after eight days His disciples were again inside, and Thomas with them. Jesus came, the doors being shut,*

and stood in the midst, and said, "Peace to you!" Then He said to Thomas, "Reach your finger here and look at My hands; and reach your hand here, and put it into My side. Do not be unbelieving, but believing."

There is an important connection to be made here. Eight days earlier, He told Mary Magdalene not to touch Him because he had "not yet ascended to the Father." Once He had ascended—been placed in the hands of God, the Priest—the whole lump became holy. See it is not about you. It is not about how good or bad you have been. It is not about what you used to be. The fact is, the first One has already been declared holy.

"While we were still sinners, Christ died for us" (Romans 5:8). He went through death, burial and resurrection to become an incorruptible body. That incorruptible body is the one Christ presents to the Father after He is raised from the dead. This is why the devil has no power over you once you come to Christ. Your spirit is put in a place where the devil is unable to touch it.

This principle was put into effect to produce the resurrection of Jesus, and is the reason why we are saved. *"For as by one man's disobedience many were made sinners, so also by one Man's obedience many will be made righteous"* (Romans 5:19). The same thing happens when you give the Firstfruit. That is the principle.

In order for your Firstfruit to ensure the resurrection of your lump—that which is attached to you and your household—it must be placed in the hands of the priest, God's representative. We are the body of Christ. When Christ committed His **spirit** into the hands of the Father, it ensured His resurrection from the grave. Likewise, when you give your life to Christ, you commit **your spirit** into the hands of the Father, becoming rescued from death, which is separation from God and eternal damnation. Christ's ascension to the Father as a presentation of His resurrected body ensured the resurrection of His lump—everything attached to Him. Once we become saved, our attachment to Him takes effect.

Therefore, all men can live because we are the sons of God and we call Him Father. Once Christ committed His newly transformed, incorruptible body into the hands of the Father, it ensured our salvation and resurrection.

You and I must do what Jesus did when His resurrected **body** ascended to the Father. We must place our offering into the hands of the priest. When you place the Firstfruit into the hands of the priest, you sanctify your entire lump—your family, your finances, your business, your health, and everything connected to your household. You put it in a place where Satan cannot touch it and it **must** be resurrected in the same manner we were resurrected because of the sacrificial offering Christ gave. It was not just a sacrifice; it was a Firstfruit offering placed in the hands of the Father and is the reason why you and I are saved today. You became a part of Christ's lump when you gave your life to Him—so you had to be delivered. But that does not ensure the deliverance of your lump. All you have to do is connect yourself with Him. When Jesus put His spirit into the hands of the Father on the cross, He assured His resurrection. When Jesus presented His resurrected body into the hands of the Father, He assured your resurrection.

No matter what had you. No matter what devil or spirit had its grip on you. No matter what afflicted your family through a generational curse, Jesus fixed it. He fixed it so every person lumped in with Him receives the same blessing. If you will put your Firstfruit in the hands of the priest, God says that no devil will be able to hold onto anything that belongs to you.

I know some of you reading this book feel like you gave the best part of your life away. Perhaps drugs took it. Perhaps alcohol took it. Perhaps a bad relationship or marriage took it. You might think it is over. But if you will put the Firstfruit in the hands of the priest, God will redeem your soul from destruction. He will restore years of your life. He will do in a few months what you thought would take years. You might say, "What is the

Firstfruit?" It is your spirit. Like Jesus gave His into the hands of the Father, you must give yours into the hands of the Father. The promise is, "Give Me your spirit, and I will make sure the rest of you follows."

****

If this revelation ministered to you, let us pray a personal prayer so that the full power of the Firstfruit principle is released in your life.

> *Master, I bless You and praise You for the truth of Your word. I want to get my life in a position to really be blessed. I want the blessing of God on my house. I thank You that I am coming into the full revelation of the power of the Firstfruit offering and that once I put it into practice, it will bring me out of lack, bondage, doubt, and fear. I thank You that as I give the Firstfruit of my increase into the hands of the priest, he shall wave it before You and command a blessing to rest not only on me, but on my entire household. I thank You Lord for Christ, the Firstfruit that has caused my lump to be holy. I thank You for restoring this truth to my life and I pray that You seal this word in my heart. I thank You in advance for the powerful breakthrough that will result in my life and I give You all the praise, in Jesus' name. Amen.*

Chapter VI

What Does Love Have to Do With It?

Everything! During prayer one day, the Spirit of the Lord instructed me to declare this truth to the people of God. As a matter of fact, a part of this teaching happened as I spoke with another believer.

A gentleman came up to me and said, "Bishop, I've heard what you taught in the word of God pertaining to the Firstfruit. I see it in God's word and I know it's the truth. I am doing exactly what you said. Yet, I have not seen the breakthrough that I am hearing other people begin to talk about." As I was standing there, the Spirit of the Lord prompted me to ask him this: "Are you harboring ill feelings toward anyone? Is there someone you need to forgive?" And he said, "Well, you know, there is something I need to handle."

I want you to understand something. I know God's word works. As you speak and do the will of God, there is a blessing on the other side. There is a reward when you do the will of God. Therefore, if we are doing God's will and not receiving a blessing or the reward for our obedience, the one thing I always settle on is that it is not God's fault. You may ask, "Now, what does that mean?" It means that if I am doing what God said to do and I am not receiving His blessing, then I cannot consider that God is not doing something. I must search myself.

The problem is never with God and you must settle this in yourself. God says if He spoke it, it is done. Let me say that again, if God spoke it, **it is done**. So if something is not working, there must be another reason.

The principal text for this chapter is Matthew 6:14-15, and it declares, *"For if you forgive men their trespasses, your heavenly*

Father will also forgive you." But if you do not forgive men their trespasses, neither will your Father forgive your trespasses." Ouch.

You may pose the question to me, "Why are you dealing with this? What does this have to do with the principle of Firstfruits giving?" I want you to notice something, and follow me through this truth. This text is at the end of Jesus' teaching on the model prayer. He just taught us how to access the presence of God by faith. He teaches us in prayer that it is the exercising of our faith that will get us into position to hear and receive from God. He instructed us to pray, "Give us this day our daily bread" and He follows that with, "And forgive us our debts as we forgive our debtors" (Matthew 6:11-12). This is key.

Of all the things Jesus articulates in the model prayer, the one thing He comes back to and reiterates in Matthew 6:14-15 is that if you do not forgive men their trespasses, then your heavenly Father will not forgive your trespasses. Jesus already said this once in Matthew 6:12 "Forgive us our debts as we forgive our debtors." But He revisits this issue because He wants us to understand that His desire to commune with us in prayer - to bless and prosper us - is about living in the kingdom dimension. This means living by the principles of the Kingdom of God. Please understand that all of these things are **principles** of God's kingdom that work by faith.

Galatians 5:6 states, *"For in Christ Jesus neither circumcision nor uncircumcision avails anything, but faith working through love."* Your faith is designed to work in a certain kind of environment. In other words, your faith will not work if you are not moving in love. Faith only works in an atmosphere or the environment of love. It will not work in an environment of hatred. It will not work in an environment of unforgiveness or offense.

For example, a car engine is made to run inside of a car, right? Now, if you submerge the entire car in water and try to start it, it will not work. Yes,

> Faith only works in the atmosphere or the environment of love.

the engine is still in the right place. But the problem is that the car is in the wrong place. It is in the wrong kind of environment for the engine to work. So it is with your faith. It may be in you, but if you are not in the right environment your faith will not work.

Make no mistake about it - the blessings of God, the dimension and the principles of the Kingdom of God will not work if you are in unforgiveness. That is what Jesus says in Matthew, chapter 6. He wants you and I to understand that unforgiveness will hinder every blessing and reward God has for you. If you do not learn how to forgive, you will come up empty because you are not in position to receive the blessing that comes with obedience.

Having said that, you need to understand that forgiveness is loving someone after they have offended you; choosing to love someone after they have hurt, wounded and treated you unjustly. I want to help you renew your mind in this area.

You might ask, "So then, what is love?" Again, the Bible says in Galatians that faith works by love—and I am sure you want your faith to work. Do you understand that if your faith does not work, you will not receive anything from God? This is because *"without faith it is impossible to please Him, for he who comes to God must believe that He is, and that He is a rewarder of those who diligently seek him"* (Hebrews 11:6).

It logically follows that if the Bible says it is impossible to please God without faith, and it also says that faith works by love; then you could say that without love, you will never please God. Faith alone will not work. Therefore, if you do not learn how to love, you will not walk in blessing. This is about you. It is not about who offended you and it is not about who hurt or wounded you. **It is about you.** Again, forgiveness is love **after** an offense. Knowing that, you must understand the principle of love.

LOVE IS A KINGDOM PRINCIPLE

Love is a set of principles established in the word of God. Love is not a feeling. I pray Christians, especially those of you reading this book, will come to understand that if you are ever going to walk in kingdom power, you must divorce yourself from living by your emotions and start living by the principles of the word of God. Neither forgiveness nor love is emotional. The Bible says, "God so **loved** the world that He gave…" (John 3:16). It does not say that God felt good about the world. It does not say He was emotionally attached to the world. In fact, if you read your Bible, you will see that by Genesis, chapter 6, God was repentant that He had ever made man.

You might ask how God could be sorry for making man and still love him. This is how: God did not allow His feelings to change His actions. He refused to allow how He felt about man to change what He promised to do for man. This is the way you and I must learn to live as children of His kingdom. I must take the position that I refuse to allow how I feel about you to change how I respond to you. My feelings are liars. God's word is truth.

> How to love your enemies:
> 1) Bless Them
> 2) Do Good by Them
> 3) Pray for Them

Jesus says in Matthew 5:44, *"But I say unto you, love your enemies, bless those who curse you, do good to those who hate you, and pray for those who spitefully use you and persecute you."* He said to **love** your enemies, which means they are still your enemies. This does not mean that you feel particularly good about them at the moment. But Jesus still says to love them.

> My feelings are liars. God's Word is truth.

How do you love your enemies? One, two, three: bless them, do good by them, and pray for them. That is it. That is love. You might think it is too simple. That is the point—it is simple!

There are three principles to loving your enemies. **The first principle is to bless them**. The word "offense" is the Greek word *scandalon* for which we get the English word *scandal*. It literally means "a trap." It is not a trap for your enemy; it is a trap for you. A trap catches you and keeps you from moving forward. That is what it is designed to do. An offense is literally a trap of the enemy. He knows if you forgive the person who offended you, you have access to your blessing. The key to accessing your blessing is to bless your enemy. The word "bless" means to *endow to prosper*. You endow your enemy to prosper by speaking God's word over their life. Release them to God. Jesus wants you to bless them. He did not say to walk on the other side of the church to avoid them. He said to bless them.

> An offense is literally a trap of the enemy.

The second principle is to do good by them. This is an action. God says to do something. In other words, do not just sit there and take it. Do not go over in your mind, "Well, I can't believe she did that." Why can't you believe it? It happened. You do not need to believe it; you need to do something about it. In other words, as you do good, this takes you to the other side of the offense.

Remember, it is just a trap! That is why every time you are about to be blessed, somebody comes and makes you angry. The enemy knows he cannot stop your faith or stop you from speaking the word. But he can stop your love. He can keep your believing and confessing from working by trapping you. Send a card, make a quick phone call. Do something that releases you and that person from the offense between you. God says you have to learn how to consistently release yourself from the traps of the enemy if you want to receive the blessings of the kingdom.

Third, pray for them. Child of God, I have learned in twenty-something years of walking with God that you cannot hate someone you are praying for. You cannot pray for them and still feel harsh toward them. You cannot do it. You may not like them when you start to pray for them, but remember, it is not about how you feel. All you have to do is pray and then God will begin to condition your heart to walk properly toward them.

So again, the principles to walking in love toward your enemy are: bless them, do good by them and pray for them. That is what Jesus instructs us to do so we do not become trapped by the offense.

FORGIVENESS IS NOT AN ADMISSION OF WRONG

This is something you must renew in your mind. One reason we do not like to ask for forgiveness is because we think forgiveness, in and of itself, is an admission of wrong. This misconception is a major stronghold. The world teaches us that asking forgiveness forces us to admit fault and claim weakness. In the Kingdom of God, asking for forgiveness has nothing to do with admitting you are wrong. On the other hand, if you are wrong you need to admit that.

Jesus teaches in Matthew 5:46-48, *"For if you love those who love you, what reward have you? Do not even the tax collectors do the same, and if you greet your brethren only what do you do more than others? Do not even the tax collectors do so? Therefore, you should be perfect* (or mature) *as your Father in heaven is perfect* (or mature).*"*

Notice what Jesus said: *"If you love those who love you, what reward have you?"* That means there is a reward for loving. When He says to love your enemies, He says this because there is a reward tied to it. It does not matter who was wrong.

Suppose you and a co-worker were in conflict with one another, and you went to ask forgiveness of him. According to the teaching in Matthew, chapter 5, you are not asking for him to forgive you because you were wrong. You are not in pursuit of being liked, justified, or excused by him. What you need to understand is that you are after a reward, and as long as there is conflict between you, that situation is in your way.

At this point, you simply need to get past it. You are on your way to the prize – the promotion, the house, the healing, the deliverance.

PEACE

Jesus says in Matthew 5:23-24, *"Therefore if you bring your gift to the altar, and there remember that your brother has something against you, leave your gift there before the altar, and go your way. First be reconciled to your brother, and then come and offer your gift."* There are several points to draw out of this scripture. As such, we will dissect it line by line.

The first point is this: Jesus says, "Therefore if you bring your gift to the altar..." One reason we bring a gift to the altar is because we expect to receive something from God. Our attitude is this: we love God and bring Him an offering because there is a reward for obeying Him.

Jesus goes on to say that if you bring your gift to the altar and you have an unreconciled conflict in your heart, leave your gift **before** the altar and go and be reconciled with them. In truth, you should have handled it before then; but if you get to the altar and the problem is still unresolved, Jesus says you must do something about it if you want Him to receive your gift.

Let us say you feel impressed to give an offering to God. You prepare it and make your way to the altar. As you approach, you feel a conviction and some type of strife between you and someone else is brought to your remembrance. If you leave a gift without having been reconciled, the church will cash the check, but God will not credit it to your heavenly account. As a result, you will not receive the blessing intended for you.

You must evaluate yourself. Jesus said if you get to the altar and "there remember that your brother has something against you...," not that you have something against your brother. This is not even about how you feel. This is actually about how you have made someone else feel. It must be reconciled.

You say, "I am doing all I know to do; I am giving my Firstfruit, I am giving my tithe, and I am giving my offering, but it is not working!" If you are not reconciled with your brother, then your gift will not produce the reward. Examine this area of your life.

Jesus continues in verse 25 with, *"Agree with your adversary quickly..."* What does Jesus mean by this? He instructs us to quickly agree with our adversaries, which means they are still our adversaries when we approach them. In other words, Jesus knows that things have not been settled between the two of you.

Jesus says to reconcile **quickly**. Ephesians 4:26 says, *"Be angry, and do not sin:* **do not let the sun go down** *on your wrath."* Do not wait a week or two weeks. The longer you wait, the harder your heart becomes and the more you begin to reason and justify your anger. You begin to say things like, "Well, I didn't do anything to her, she did it to me. She should be coming to me." What you fail to understand when you do this is that malice begins to settle in your spirit and it becomes like roaches crawling all over you, eating you alive.

While you are trying to justify yourself, you are losing ground. While you are reasoning, you are losing ground. While you are mumbling, you are losing ground. While you are deciding who is going to be first to apologize, you are losing ground. God says the reason you fight it is because you think asking for forgiveness is an admission of wrong. It has nothing to do with that.

If you continue on in that same passage, Jesus goes on to say, *"Agree with your adversary quickly, while you are on the way with him, lest your adversary deliver you to the judge, the judge hand you over to the officer, and you be thrown into prison"* (Matthew 5:25). He is not just talking about prison here, Jesus is referring to spirits.

Do not miss this vital point. Jesus said when you first begin (when you are initially angry) you are only confronting a little spirit.

> You cannot collect rewards in prison.

But if you continue to entertain him, he will turn you over to a judge because he has you now, and you no longer fight to be released. Anger will turn you over to a heavier devil, like depression; and then depression will turn you over to another spirit, like uncleanness. Let us be real here. Some of you cannot stop fornicating because you are in unforgiveness. It is not that you are not saved or that you do not love God. It is that a judge has turned you over to an officer.

And you fail to understand and recognize that the enemy has a legal right to hold you and throw you into prison. Jesus goes on to say in Matthew 5:26, *"Assuredly, I say to you, you will by no means get out of there till you have paid the last penny."* We all know that Jesus will never lie and Jesus will never deceive us. He says, assuredly you are going to pay. That does not only mean financially. You pay with your time, with your emotions, you even pay with your soul. Jesus says you will not come out of there until you have paid the uttermost authority and the highest amount because you are legally held there by your own will. The blessing of the kingdom is withheld from you. You cannot collect rewards in prison.

Jesus teaches us here that forgiveness has nothing to do with who was wronged. What forgiveness absolutely has to do with is who wants to be blessed first, and who wants to be blessed most. The reason I ask for your forgiveness is not because I think I did something wrong. I ask for your forgiveness because I want to be blessed.

You might be thinking, "Is that legal? I should ask for forgiveness because I am sorry." Jesus did not say be sorry; He said love. Who told you that you needed to be sorry? That did not come from the word of God. Now, if you want to believe it, then fine. However, if it did not come from the Word, you do not have to believe it and you do not have to agree with it. Jesus did not say you needed to be sorry. He instructed you and me to love.

You might pose the question then, "If asking for forgiveness has nothing to do with admitting that I am wrong, what does it have to do with? Child of God, it has to do with peace and prosperity. I ask for forgiveness because I do not want to be tormented by judges or officers and become their prisoner. I need peace. I do not want to open myself up to devils because of a conflict with you.

Secondly, it has to do with prosperity. As long as you stay in this position, you are not going to receive payment; you are going to pay. Nothing in the Kingdom of God will work for you if you do not renew your mind in this area. Forgiveness is about peace and prosperity on your life. This is not about who did who wrong. If there is someone to whom you need to be reconciled, do it quickly. Jesus said to agree with your adversary quickly. He did not say to agree quickly when your adversary becomes a friend.

> Forgiveness is about peace and prosperity.

Husband, wife, friend, foe, mother, or father, it does not matter. If you can forgive that individual, then you will be blessed, prospered and in peace. If the person who wronged you is no longer living, that does not make any difference. There is not anything you can do for them, but it is not about them. This is about you and your release.

Here is what I have learned. If that person is no longer alive, then you should do what David did when Saul tried to pin David to the wall with a javelin. David could no longer do anything good for him because Saul was dead. The Scripture records in 1 Samuel 18:11, *"And Saul cast the spear; for he said, 'I will pin David to the wall!' but David escaped his presence twice."* David said in 2 Samuel 9:1, *"Is there still anyone who is left of the house of Saul, that I may show him kindness for Jonathan's sake?"*

This was not something David just wanted to do. He understood that he needed to get that offense off him. And so, David went to one of Saul's children, Mephiboshet, and set him at the table of the king and said, *"As long as this one lives, he will be taken care of by me."* David knew he needed to keep that area of his heart right before God.

If that person is deceased, then I urge you to find someone in their family and send them a card. Write them and say, "I am praying for you." This will bring such healing and release to your life. This is a principle of God's Word.

****

Father, in Jesus' name, I pray that this word find its right place in the heart of those for whom You have intended. I pray in the name of Jesus that You would give my brother or sister the power to release themselves from the prison of the judge and the officer. In the name of Jesus Christ of Nazareth, I open the trap by the anointing and the power of the Word of God. And, in the name of Jesus, I decree the release of that which has been withheld, and the release of those who have been held by unforgiveness. Wherever it is, wherever it came from, I expose you devil. You can no longer hold my brother and my sister. You can no longer hold them.

I lead them in the prayer of release, forgiveness and repentance. Lord, some of them have been wronged. They did nothing wrong. They were on the sharp end of the sword that was pointed toward them through no fault of their own, but it still cut and it hurt.

Child of God, pray this prayer with me:

Lord, in the name of Jesus, I forgive and I release this individual who hurt me, who wounded me, who scarred me. I give them to you and I ask your forgiveness. If I have been responsible for doing the same thing to any brother or sister: Forgive me, and I forgive them. In the name of Jesus, I receive the blessing of peace and the reward of prosperity. I declare that everything that is supposed to come to me is released right now, and it is on its way to me. I am released. I am released in Jesus' name.

If there is an individual you need to forgive, call their name out to God. Nobody has to know but you must deal with this thing before God. Tell Him, "God, I give them to you, I release them to you. Whatever I can do for them, tell me."

Remember my friend, faith works by love. Forgive and receive the blessing of God on your life.

CHAPTER VII

MAKE YOUR DREAMS COME TRUE

In the first three chapters we discussed God's dream for your life, actions you need to take to move into those dreams, and obstacles you will face as you take possession of them. In chapters four and five we covered the main concept of this book in great detail – the principle of Firstfruit giving as a vital but often missing key to our financial covenant with God. Chapter 6 examined how walking in love and forgiveness provides the atmosphere for the manifestation of God's dream in our lives. In this final chapter, I want to talk about evidence of the dream.

Hope is the evidence of your dream until it manifests in the physical realm. It has to do with that which is not seen. The Bible says: *"For we were saved in this hope, but hope that is seen is not hope; for why does one still hope for what he sees?"* (Romans 8:24). When the writer says "hope that is seen is not hope," he is talking about hope that is not yet perceptible to the senses. This is not limited to sight but refers to all the senses. In the same manner that the Bible says, *"For we walk by faith, not by sight"* (2 Corinthians 5:7), it not only refers to your natural vision, but it talks about your sensory perception as well. If you walk by faith you do not walk by what you see, what you hear, or what you can touch. Faith removes you from the realm of your natural senses. You see your hopes and dreams in the spirit, but they have not physically manifested. As a matter of fact, close your eyes right now and picture your dream. When you see it, open your eyes. With your eyes open, do you still see your dream? No. My point is that you see your dreams and hopes in your mind because they exist in your spirit. When you open your eyes you do not see them because they have no substance.

The Bible says, *"...faith is the substance of things hoped for..."* (Hebrews 11:1) which tells me that hope has no substance. Something that has substance is tangible or touchable. So, faith is the material of my hopes and dreams. Faith gives my hope or my dream tangibility.

> Hopes and dreams are not tangible. FAITH gives them substance.

Faith makes my dream touchable in the material realm. Because I cannot actually touch my hopes and dreams in the physical realm, I must give them physical qualities. My faith is the evidence, the proof that my dream exists. Proof is a visible manifestation, materialization or truth.

In order to know what faith actually means, we need a working definition of it – what God means when He refers to faith. James 2:14-18 provides this definition. It reads:

> *What does it profit, my brethren, if someone says he has faith but does not have works? Can faith save him? If a brother or sister is naked and destitute of daily food, and one of you says to them, "Depart in peace, be warmed and filled," but you do not give them the things which are needed for the body, what does it profit? Thus also faith by itself, if it does not have works is dead. But someone will say, "You have faith, and I have works." Show me your faith without your works, and I will show you my faith by my works."*

In other words, I will show you what I believe by what I do. Verse 18 shows us that faith – Bible faith – is a conviction or persuasion

> **Bible Faith** is a conviction or persuasion *plus* a corresponding action.

plus a corresponding action. What I believe – my conviction or persuasion – alone is not Bible faith. The belief in you is not Bible faith until it can be heard or seen. Therefore, if faith is the substance and serves as proof of your hope or dream, and faith is conviction or persuasion plus corresponding action, then conviction or persuasion plus corresponding action is the proof that your dream exists. You need to know this in order to make your dream come true.

Let us look at the story of Joseph as an example. Joseph was the dreamer. He was the one who saw his brothers bowing down to him as a young boy and saw visions that would indeed come to pass. When Joseph's brothers sold him into slavery, he went to Potiphar's house and became second in command. Joseph was sent to prison because Potiphar's wife falsely accused him of seducing her. Upon his release, he was promoted to second in command to Pharaoh. He was the one who, through the spirit of revelation and wisdom, gained insight from interpreting Pharaoh's dream that Egypt should store corn because a famine was to come upon the earth. As a result of Joseph's revelation, Egypt was the only place on the earth where there was food. This was due to the wisdom of a man of God who was able to see what others could not see.

The famine led Joseph's brothers to Egypt – the only place one could buy food. Thinking he was dead, they did not know who Joseph was when they saw him, but he recognized them. It was then that Joseph's dream – the vision he had seen – was fulfilled. They bowed down to him. With authority and power to preserve them, Joseph said, *"...God sent me before you to preserve life"* (Genesis 45:5). Joseph was put in place when his brothers sold him into slavery, they meant it for evil, but God meant it for good. The same is true in your life. God knows you have to be in place for something. The person who comes against you may mean their actions for evil, but God means them for good.

In Genesis 50:22-25, Joseph the dreamer gives the children of Israel one final dream from his deathbed. He declares that God will visit them in Egypt, and when He does, He will deliver them. The children of Israel were to carry Joseph's bones with them to God. Joseph foresaw trouble for Israel that he had never actually experienced. He prophesied a vision they could not comprehend.

> *So Joseph dwelt in Egypt, he and his father's household. And Joseph lived one hundred and ten years. Joseph saw Ephraim's children to the third generation... And Joseph said to his brethren, "I am dying; but God will surely visit you, and bring you out of this land to the land of which he swore to Abraham, to Isaac, and to Jacob." Then Joseph took an oath from the children of Israel, saying, "God will surely visit you, and you shall carry up my bones from here"* (Genesis 50:22-25).

Exodus 1 details the history of the Israelite bondage in Egypt. *"Now, there arose a new king over Egypt, who did not know Joseph"* (Exodus 1:8). At this point, Joseph the Israelite is dead. He was second in command to the previous pharaoh, but this new ruler had no concern for him. He did not know what Joseph did or how he helped during the famine. He had no regard for Joseph, but he grew concerned with the strength of the children of Israel. This new pharaoh says in verses 9-12 of the same chapter:

> *"Look, the people of the children of Israel are more and mightier than we; come, let us deal shrewdly with them, lest they multiply, and it happen, in the event of war, that they also join our enemies and fight against us, and so go up out of the land." Therefore they set taskmasters over them to afflict them with their burdens. And they built for Pharaoh supply cities, Pithom and Raamses. But the more they afflicted them, the more they multiplied and grew. And they were in dread of the children of Israel.*

It is the same for you as you begin to walk into your dream. As you grow stronger, the enemy fears you may gain too much power. As we discussed in chapter 1, great opposition often verifies great promise.

Remember, Joseph was the dreamer; but as we discussed before, dreams have no substance. He prophesied the children of

Israel's deliverance, but the promise needed tangibility in the physical realm. As I brought to your attention previously, Joseph made them swear an oath to carry his bones to the Lord. Because this was an oath – an oral agreement – he made them say back to him what he prophesied and instructed them to do. That is how you swear an oath.

This oath is what propelled them into their dream. When the Israelites get word that they are free, they are on their way to the land God swore to Abraham, Isaac and Jacob. It is evident to them that God is performing His word, keeping His word, and the children of Israel are preparing to walk into their dream. However, in order to walk into their dream, they must go get Joseph's bones, because they swore they would take his bones with them. Exodus 13:17-19 declares:

> *Then it came to pass, when Pharaoh had let the people go, that God did not lead them by way of the land of the Philistines, although that was near; for God said, "Lest perhaps the people change their minds when they see war, and return to Egypt." So God led the people around by way of the wilderness of the Red Sea. And the children of Israel went up in orderly ranks out of the land of Egypt. And Moses took the bones of Joseph with him, for he had placed the children of Israel under solemn oath, saying, "God will surely visit you, and you shall carry my bones from here with you."*

Joseph's bones represented the materiality of the dream. His bones were the evidence. As the children of Israel carried Joseph's bones, they carried the substance of that which they hoped for, and the evidence of the thing that they had not yet seen—deliverance. Get this! The bones represented the oath they swore to Joseph. The oath is the word. **Faith is the evidence.**

These things are written for your example, and to show you how you are to fulfill God's purpose for your life. God is telling you that if you want to walk into your dream, then you must have evidence that your dream exists. There must be material of the dream. I have told you about the oath they swore to Joseph in which they promised to carry his bones. 2 Corinthians 4:13 reads: *"...we also believe and therefore speak..."* This means that if you want to walk into your dream, you have to carry the oath – the promise God swore to you – and say it back to Him. You must put Him in remembrance of His word.

You cannot simply believe. The giving of your Firstfruit, tithe, and devoted offering is mandatory for moving into your dream dimension; but you must speak what God told you with every step you take. Carry your bones! This is your evidence. It is the corresponding action that goes with your conviction or persuasion. So what if you look silly calling yourself a millionaire or claiming your blessing! That is how you walk into your dream! You must say back to God what God has said to you. If He said it belongs to you, **you** say it belongs to you.

> To walk into your dream, you must say to God what He has said to you. If He said it belongs to you, **you** say it belongs to you.

Joseph's dream was just like your dream; it had no substance to the children of Israel when he spoke it. It was not tangible at that point. He spoke Israel's deliverance from Egypt **before** it happened. It was already done in the spiritual realm, but the power of true faith needed to be released in the natural realm. You must carry the oath that God made to you, so that He can hear it. You must provide some tangibility to your dream if you are going to walk in what God promised you. How do you do that? By the oath. What is an oath? It is a promise. It is the proof that your dream is real.

****

Father, in the magnificence of Your Word, You have unfolded the mystery of how we walk into our dreams. You do not make our dreams happen, but You show them to us. We understand that we must carry the bones, the structure, the material of our dreams. I pray in the name of Jesus that You would cause Your oath, Your promise, Your word to come into the heart and mouth of your child because their dream will not come to pass simply because they see it. It will come to pass because they keep their covenant of Firstfruit, tithe, and offering and carry the oath.

The dream will not come to pass because You made it, it will come to pass because somebody is speaking Your word. You said You would provide, and so we say, "You are providing." You said You would heal us, and so we say, "We are healed." You said You would make a way, and so we declare, "You have made a way." And so, as we walk by faith, we do not say, "It will be done." We say, "It is done!" And as we say it is, we understand that, to others, we look crazy carrying bones. We know that it does not make sense in the natural to carry bones, but we are not trying to make sense, we are believing to make faith. Father, in the name of Jesus, I release the anointing of God to make dreams a reality.

Now Father, your people will walk in the revelation of this truth, and as they do, bring material to their dream. By your power, I decree that they are walking in what you have shown them, and the devil cannot stop it. In the name of Jesus, Amen!

My brother, my sister, I declare that the God who you have been waiting for has been waiting for you to pick up the bones and carry them. I declare that the power you have been waiting for, you have the authority to release by the Word of God.

BISHOP CLARENCE E. MCCLENDON, PH.D..

Clarence E. McClendon was born and raised in Decatur, Illinois and began preaching at age fifteen. He assumed his first pastorate at age nineteen and today serves as the Senior Pastor of Full Harvest International, a rapidly growing global, multi-cultural congregation. Dr. McClendon is also the Founder and President of the Siloam Bible College and Clarence E. McClendon Leadership Institute, dedicated to training 21st Century leaders of today with a vision for tomorrow; *Kingdom Harvest Ministries, Inc.*, and *Clarence E. McClendon Ministries*, Inc., which are enterprises that encompass weekly national and international broadcasts and international ministry crusades. Currently more than 160 million homes have access to Harvest Fire broadcasts throughout North America, Europe, Africa, South America, and the Middle East. In addition, nearly one million people have been ministered to via Harvest Fire Crusades. Bishop McClendon also hosts an annual conference that draws in excess of 40,000 people to Los Angeles each summer.

Dr. McClendon serves on the Bishop's Council of the Full Gospel Baptist Church Fellowship in charge of Fellowship Relations, and he has accepted a seat on the College of Bishops of the International Communion of Charismatic Churches. Both of these associations are interdenominational fellowships where he continues to build a reputation as a force for reconciliation and harmony across ethnic, denominational, generational, and geographic lines.

He also serves as a board member of the *Do Something* Foundation, a think-tank of some of America's top young leaders, and as a California Regent for President Bush's Faith Based Initiative Faith Center.

As a voice of authority regarding some of society's most pressing issues, he has appeared on the CBS *Evening News* with Dan Rather, *Nightline* on ABC and *Black Entertainment Television*.

As an accomplished author, he has penned *The X Blessing, Beyond Personal Power: Experiencing the God Kind of Faith and And When You Pray: The Key to Accessing the Presence of God.* His musical accolades include the Stellar Award nominated CD "Shout Hallelujah" which debuted on the Billboard's top ten listing for gospel music.

Other Materials Available by Clarence E. McClendon Ministries

Books:

X Blessing
And When You Pray
Beyond Personal Power: Experiencing the "God-Kind of Faith"

Audio Tape Series:

Reversing A Cursing
Seeds to Your Success
Coming Into A Wealthy Place
The Power to Get Wealth

CLARENCE E. MCCLENDON MINISTRIES
P.O. BOX 78398
LOS ANGELES, CALIFORNIA 90016

FOR MORE INFORMATION PLEASE VISIT
WWW.CEMM.INFO